THIRD AND A MILE

THIRD AND A MILE

THE TRIALS AND TRIUMPHS OF THE BLACK QUARTERBACK

WILLIAM C. RHODEN

ISBN-13: 978-1-933060-11-8
ISBN-10: 1-933060-11-5

ESPN books are available for special promotions and premiums. For details contact Michael Rentas, Assistant Director, Inventory Operations, Hyperion, 77 West 66th Street, 11th floor, New York, New York 10023, or call 212-456-0133.

FIRST EDITION

10 9 8 7 6 5 4 3 2 1

ESPN BOOKS
a division of
ESPN publishing

To Sharon and Raisa, as always.
To all of those black Field Generals, past and present,
who faced Third and a Mile with
valor, grace, and courage.

CONTENTS

MOVING THE CHAINS

Third and a Mile officially started for me in July 2005, at a meeting in Atlanta. After months of schedule wrangling, I was finally sitting face-to-face with a group of legendary men known as the Field Generals—James Harris, Marlin Briscoe, Doug Williams, and Warren Moon—and though it was our first get-together, it seemed as if we'd known each other for years.

In fact, we had.

My history with the Field Generals is a long one.

I first crossed paths with James "Shack" Harris at Yankee Stadium in 1968. I was a freshman defensive back at Morgan State, and he was an All-America quarterback at Grambling. Our schools met in what was billed as a battle of the titans of Black College Football. Grambling was the defending national champion among black colleges. Morgan hadn't lost a game in three years. In front of a sellout crowd of 64,204, Morgan won the game 9–7 with a goal-line stand as time expired.

Shack Harris, described by one writer as "the best thing out of the South since hominy grits," was injured, but he came off the bench late in the fourth quarter and moved the Tigers seventy-seven yards in three minutes. What most impressed me about Shack was how he completed each pass with strength and authority. Alabama A&M quarterback Onree Jackson was also a highly regarded pro prospect that year, but scouts predicted that Shack would be the first African-American quarterback to make it big in the National Football League.

They were right. Harris very nearly led the Los Angeles Rams to the Super Bowl and he was named MVP of the Pro Bowl. Later, after retiring from the NFL as a player, Harris rose through the scouting ranks to become vice president of player personnel for the Jacksonville Jaguars.

Marlin Briscoe and I met in 1974, the year I joined *Ebony* magazine. My first assignment was to write and edit a pro football roundup. The theme was "African-American Quarterbacks: One Foot in the Door." Shack Harris had locked up the starting job in LA that season, and Joe Gilliam—the indomitable Jefferson Street Joe from Tennessee State—had bested Terry Bradshaw for the starting position in Pittsburgh. Briscoe, who only six years earlier had become the first African-American to start an American Football League game at quarterback, for the Denver Broncos, was one of the first people I contacted for reaction to the news.

As for Doug Williams and Warren Moon, I had spoken with them numerous times these last twenty years as a sportswriter and columnist for *The New York Times*.

What occurred to me as I listened to the stories that afternoon, two years ago in Atlanta, was that I could just as easily be listening to a group of black CEOs discussing the challenges in their respective occupations. The frustrations, the barriers, the prejudices that the Field Generals encountered were all too familiar to African-Americans. They were simply being played out on a more public stage.

As with all civil rights struggles, the battle to integrate the quarterback position stirred passions. What's unique about it is that the debate raged on long after every other position in the four major sports had been opened to African-American athletes.

Why?

Well, no other position requires so much of one person. Not goalie in hockey, not point guard or center in basketball, not pitcher or catcher in baseball. In the hearts and minds of hard-core football fans, the quarterback is the epitome of leadership, the CEO, the true Big Man on Campus.

More than on physical prowess, a quarterback succeeds—or fails—on his core intelligence, mental agility, and football judgment. He's constantly being tested on his ability to make sense of the scrambled information he picks up in the eight to ten seconds between barking, "Break!" in the huddle, receiving the snap, and getting rid of the football.

If, say, a defensive back lines up in position B instead of position A as expected, how rapidly can the quarterback race through his catalog of alternatives and come up with a new plan of attack?

And if that quarterback isn't sufficiently astute to redirect the efforts of ten teammates in a split second, how can he inspire, how can he manage, how can he *lead* his team?

Ours is a sporting culture with room for a diversity of roles, heroes of all shapes and sizes. But add race to the mix, and suddenly you discover that African-Americans are found wanting.

Critics—okay, *white* critics—allow that African-American athletes have "soul," that black folks can get out there and "make things happen," that we are "athletic." But capable of rational thought under pressure? Split-second judgments? The ability to take command and deliver the goods?

Not so fast.

Somehow, all the leadership traits embodied by a great quarterback are perceived to be beyond the reach of a quarterback with a black face. At least that's the way it was when the great football players whose voices you'll hear in this book fought to explode the conventional wisdom that black men are all brawn and no brains, "natural athletes" rather than smart, self-taught leaders.

In 1971, according to Harry J. Knopke, Robert J. Norrell, and Ronald W. Rogers, authors of *Opening Doors: Perspectives on Race Relations in Contemporary America*, Hall of Fame quarterback Fran Tarkenton summed up the argument like this:

> *"As for quarterback, it doesn't take more than a few seconds of glancing at the NFL roster to figure out that the vast majority of them are Anglo-Saxons…By tradition, Anglo-Saxons have been prideful, explorative, curious men with a powerful strain of self-confidence. These characteristics have been developed over centuries of family life and schooling, and Anglo-Saxons seem to be ethnically well equipped to operate as leaders. On the other hand, the hatred and cultural isolation meted out to the black man over the past centuries seem to*

have provided an environment far removed from that in which cocky quarterback types are fostered. Therefore, as the black community gains confidence in itself (which is happening at an ever-accelerating rate), it should begin to raise the fund of whip-cracking personalities who can ramrod around a collection of diverse personalities like a football team. So far, for better or for worse, the Anglo-Saxon seems best equipped—culturally, not physically—for this job."

Doug Williams was the MVP of Super Bowl XXII in 1988. Steve McNair steered the Tennessee Titans to the Super Bowl in 2000. Donovan McNabb and Michael Vick went head-to-head in the NFC championship game in 2005. And Warren Moon was voted into the Hall of Fame in 2006.

Does this mean that African-Americans have finally gained the confidence of a nation?

Or does it merely mean that the financial realities of the modern-day NFL have made it unprofitable to overlook conspicuous talent?

*   *   *

After our meeting in Atlanta, Harris, Williams and I shared a cab to the airport. The driver, an African-American man in his late forties or early fifties, immediately recognized the MVP of Super Bowl XXII. "Doug Williams!" he practically shouted as he scrambled for a piece of paper for an autograph. "Aw, *man!*"

The entire ride was illuminated by his joy. All these years later, the man was visibly buoyed by what had taken place on January 31, 1988, the day Williams made history as the first black quarterback to lead an NFL team to victory in the Super Bowl. In one astonishing quarter of football, Williams had rallied the Washington Redskins past the Denver Broncos with four touchdown passes. The driver went on and on about what that performance meant to him, giving us a play-by-play rehash of the game.

For African-Americans of a certain generation, that Super Bowl win ranks right up there with Joe Louis's beating Max Schmeling in 1938 and Jackie Robinson's integrating Major League Baseball in 1947. They remember exactly where they were and exactly what they were doing when it happened.

In upstaging Denver's John Elway on that January day, Williams ended all debate about whether a black man was smart enough to play the position. At least we thought so at the time.

"That's the impact that white America doesn't understand," Williams says. "We thought it would open the floodgates for African-American quarterbacks. The fact that it didn't reflects a common history—decades of hope held out and hope denied."

In many ways, the journey of the African-American quarterback parallels the journey of all African-Americans since the dawn of U.S. history. The position itself is a metaphor for privilege, a symbol of respect, and a mark of authority, the denial of which is deeply rooted in this nation's history of liberty and justice for…some.

For two centuries and counting, African-Americans have tested the quality and depth of America's loyalty to its professed values. And America, for the most part, has consistently failed that test.

This is why the story of Joe Gilliam, the prince of Black College Football, resonated for Field Generals young and old. Jefferson Street Joe emerged from a generation of African-Americans—my generation—raised to believe that they were good enough, smart enough, strong enough to do anything.

This was *our* time.

Intelligent and solidly middle class, an accomplished gymnast and a competitive swimmer, Gilliam played quarterback at Tennessee State from 1969 to 1971, where he broke every major school passing record. During the strike-marred 1974 NFL season, Jefferson Street Joe started at quarterback for the Pittsburgh Steelers. He kept the job through six games—even after Terry Bradshaw returned—and led the Steelers to a record of 4–1–1. He knew from the get-go that he was on a short leash. "I don't plan on doing any losing," he told me during a 1974 interview for *Ebony*. "It won't take much."

Turns out he was right. Despite his winning record, Gilliam went to the bench. Bradshaw took over and led the Steelers to a Super Bowl victory.

*   *   *

During that first meeting, the Field Generals explained that after attending a memorial banquet honoring Jefferson Street Joe in 2001, they had dedicated themselves to teaching and preserving the history of the African-American quarterback for future generations.

"We want to have a better line of communication with the guys who are playing the game," Moon explained. "Not to tell them how we made it possible for them to get what they're getting, but to be a sounding board, a place where they can come to share experiences that we might be able to help them with."

The struggle hasn't ended. There have been a number of reminders recently, lingering signs of the challenges that still confront black men who elect to play the most demanding position in team sports.

In 2003, right-wing political commentator Rush Limbaugh, hired to be a lightning rod on ESPN's pregame football show, earned his money by accusing the media of propping up Donovan McNabb because it wanted an African-American to succeed at quarterback. Funny, I don't remember hearing before he made that remark—or since, for that matter—that Limbaugh knows his butt from a hole in the ground about football. But that didn't matter. He made his point, which had everything to do with politics and nothing to do with football.

Now fast forward to January 2006, when the University of Southern California and the University of Texas squared off in the Rose Bowl for the national championship. Leading the Trojans was All-America quarterback Matt Leinart, a smart field general and an exceptionally accurate pocket passer. Spearheading the Longhorns was another All-America quarterback, Vince Young, who in addition to being a smart field general did not hesitate to run with the ball when his passing options broke down.

Much like Doug Williams' Super Bowl win in 1988 had validated that an African-American quarterback had what it took to be the very best, Young's transcendent victory in his duel with Leinart raised the hopes of black Americans.

For a while, anyway.

In a turn of events that many observers—including yours truly—saw as an attempt to discredit Young (and, by extension, all

African-American quarterbacks), news was leaked two months before the NFL draft that he had scored poorly on the Wonderlic Personnel Test. Administered to prospective picks since 1968, the Wonderlic is a twelve-minute, fifty-question exam used to assess aptitude for absorbing new information and solving problems in a wide range of occupations.

Young was an excellent athlete, wrote one cynic, but his ability to function in a pro system was now called into question by his Wonderlic score. The inference was clear: For all his wonderful gifts, Young made more plays with his body than with his mind.

In the end at least, justice prevailed: When the dust settled, and NFL teams had to vote with their wallets, the Tennessee Titans took Young with the third pick in the draft. Matt Leinart went to the Cardinals at number ten.

*   *   *

This book honors the generations of African-American football players who were denied the opportunity to compete at a position that they were supremely qualified to play: quarterback.

Third and a Mile is a record of their struggle and their victory.

As Warren Moon explained, the hope is that it will become not only a source of history—"an educational tool for young quarterbacks"—but also a means of therapy, a way finally to air "some stuff we've been holding inside for too long."

From Fritz Pollard in the 1920s to Vince Young today, the link between African-American quarterbacks remains strong. Strong too is the resistance that black quarterbacks still face. Despite all the proof to the contrary—despite the wondrous achievements of black quarterbacks in the NFL over the last four decades—doubt persists.

But with an expanding network of skilled black men playing the position, we have the makings of a powerful black institution: Field Generals on the field and off.

* * *

In the course of that 1974 interview for *Ebony*, Joe Gilliam made another statement I will never forget. Speaking about the opportunity to start for the Steelers, he said: "There are two types of opportunities in professional athletics—a chance and a nigger chance." Back then, that was the dilemma every black quarterback faced.

Today the view from the huddle is much different.

When we first started floating ideas for the title for this book, Warren Moon remarked, "Third and a Mile? That's a hard one to make."

Incredibly, each successive generation of Field Generals has converted it: Wilmeth Sidat-Singh, Willie Thrower, George Taliaferro, Sandy Stephens, Marlin Briscoe, James Harris, Doug Williams, Warren Moon, Donovan McNabb, Daunte Culpepper, Michael Vick, and now Vince Young.

The next generation of Field Generals has been given a precious gift—a fresh set of downs.

For the next generation, it's First and Ten.

VOICES

Mike Adamle is a TV commentator and former running back for the Chiefs, Jets, and Bears. He played from 1971 to 1976.

Danny Barrett was a starting quarterback in the CFL and at the University of Cincinnati. He was also the head coach of the Saskatchewan Roughriders.

Skip Bayless was a longtime sports columnist in Dallas, Chicago, Miami, and Los Angeles. He has written three books on the Dallas Cowboys and is now a co-host of ESPN's *Cold Pizza*.

George Blanda played twenty-six seasons in the NFL as a quarterback and kicker for the Bears, Colts, Oilers, and Raiders. He is a member of the Pro Football Hall of Fame.

Rocky Bleier was a Steelers running back and part of their four Super Bowl-winning teams. He is now a motivational speaker.

Roy Blount Jr., a former editor at *Sports Illustrated*, is the author of nineteen books, including *About Three Bricks Shy of a Load*, which chronicled the start of the Pittsburgh Steelers dynasty.

Todd Boyd, a professor of critical studies at the University of Southern California, is the author of, among other books, *Young, Black, Rich, and Famous: The Rise of the NBA, the Hip Hop Invasion, and the Transformation of American Culture* and *Am I Black Enough for You? Popular Culture from the Hood and Beyond*.

Marlin Briscoe became the AFL's first starting African-American quarterback, in 1968, with the Denver Broncos. He went on to play nine seasons in the pros, primarily at wide receiver, and in 1970, he was elected to the Pro Bowl. He won two Super Bowls with Miami and was on the Dolphins team that went undefeated. He now is the coach of Wilson High School in Long Beach, California, runs his own football camp for young people, and is one of the founders of the Field Generals.

Kevin Carroll is the author of *Rules of the Red Rubber Ball: Find and Sustain Your Life's Work*. The founder of the Katalyst Consultancy, Carroll is a motivational speaker who has advised business leaders at Nike, Starbucks, and the Discovery Channel. Before that he was head athletic trainer for the Philadelphia 76ers.

Al Conway, an NFL umpire, was part of the officiating crew of Super Bowl XXII.

Daunte Culpepper was the number-one pick of the Minnesota Vikings in the 1999 draft. He quarterbacked the Vikings for six seasons and was Pro Bowl selection in three of those. He is now with the Miami Dolphins.

Randall Cunningham quarterbacked sixteen seasons in the NFL with the Eagles, Vikings, Cowboys, and Ravens. He was a Pro Bowler four times, and in 1989, he was voted MVP of the Pro Bowl. He is also one of the founders of the Field Generals.

Bill Curry is an ESPN college football analyst and a former Pro Bowl NFL center. He was the head coach at Georgia Tech, Alabama, and Kentucky. He is the executive director of Leadership Baylor at the Baylor School in Chattanooga, Tennessee.

Willie Davis graduated from Grambling University and was an NFL defensive lineman for twelve years. From 1960 to 1969, he was a member of the Green Bay Packer dynasty. Davis never missed a game in his pro career, played in five straight Pro Bowls, and is a member of the Pro Football Hall of Fame.

Al Denson was a Denver Broncos wide receiver from 1964 to 1970 and was a Pro Bowl selection twice. He also played one season with the Minnesota Vikings.

Judge Dickson was a fullback at the University of Minnesota and was part of the team that won the 1960 Big Ten championship and the 1962 Rose Bowl. He was also Sandy Stephens' roommate.

Jim Dooley was a wide receiver with the Chicago Bears from 1952 to 1961. He was the head coach of the Bears from 1968 to 1971.

Fred Dryer was an NFL defensive lineman for thirteen seasons, from 1969 to 1981. In 1975, he was elected to the Pro Bowl while a member of the Los Angles Rams, where he played for ten years. Also an actor, he has appeared in numerous movies and television shows.

Tony Dungy played quarterback at the University of Minnesota and was a defensive back in the NFL for three seasons, including 1978 when he played with the Super Bowl-winning Pittsburgh Steelers. He was the head coach of the Tampa Bay Buccaneers from 1996 to 2001, and since 2002, he has been the head coach of the Indianapolis Colts.

Chuck Ealey won thirty-five straight games while quarterbacking the University of Toledo from 1969 to 1971. He played quarterback for three CFL teams and was the 1972 CFL Rookie of the Year and MVP of the Grey Cup. Today, he is a business leader in Ontario.

Harry Edwards is professor emeritus of sociology at the University of California at Berkeley. He is the author of, among others, *Educating Black Athletes*.

Vince Evans was the Chicago Bears' sixth-round draft pick in 1977 after quarterbacking the USC Trojans. He played in Chicago for seven years, before moving to the USFL, and then to the Raiders for the last eight years of his career. He retired at age forty. He is one of the founders of the Field Generals.

Tom Friend is a senior writer at *ESPN The Magazine*. He covered the Redskins for *The Washington Post* from 1987 to 1989.

Charles Garcia was a teammate of Choo Choo Brackins' at Prairie View A&M.

Nelson George is a novelist and cultural critic. He was a columnist for the *Village Voice* and the author of numerous nonfiction books, including *Elevating the Game: Black Men in Basketball* and *Buppies, B-Boys, Baps, and Bohos: Notes on Post-Soul Black Culture.*

Jimmie Giles was a four-time Pro Bowl tight end during his thirteen-year career. He caught passes from both Doug Williams and Randall Cunningham. He is now the head of his own financial firm, based in Tampa, Florida.

Joe Gilliam Sr. spent forty years coaching in the college ranks, most of those with Tennessee State. He is the author of three books on football tactics.

Ernest Givins was a ten-year NFL vet, starring for the Houston Oilers from 1986 to 1995. He was a two-time Pro-Bowl selection.

Joe Greene played thirteen seasons in the NFL, from 1969 to 1981, all of them for the Pittsburgh Steelers. The defensive lineman won four Super Bowls and was a ten-time Pro Bowler. He was the NFL Defensive Player of the Year in 1972 and 1974. He is a member of the Pro Football Hall of Fame.

Dale Hamer was an NFL official for twenty-three seasons. He was the head linesman in Super Bowl XXII.

Glenn Harris is a sports anchor in Washington DC. He hosts *Sports Talk*, a nightly call-in show on News Channel 8 in the DC area.

James Harris was an NFL quarterback for ten years, from 1969 to 1979, after starring at Grambling. In 1975, he played in the Pro Bowl, where he was voted MVP. He has held several front office jobs in the NFL and is currently vice president of player personnel for the Jacksonville Jaguars. He is also one of the founders of the Field Generals.

Wilburn Hollis was the quarterback for the University of Iowa from 1959 to 1961.

Condredge Holloway attended the University of Tennessee, where he was the first African-American quarterback in the SEC. In 1974, he was the MVP of the Hula Bowl. In 1975, he was selected in the twelfth round of the NFL draft by the New England Patriots, but later that season he joined the Ottawa Rough Riders and helped them win the 1976 Grey Cup.

Ernie Holmes was a defensive lineman from 1972 to 1977 for the Pittsburgh Steelers, where he won two Super Bowls. In 1986, Holmes appeared in WrestleMania 2.

Jerry Izenberg, a sports columnist for *The Newark Star-Ledger*, is the author of several books and has won numerous awards. Izenberg also produced the documentary *Grambling College: 100 Yards to Glory*.

Harold Jackson was drafted by the Los Angeles Rams in the twelfth round out of Jackson State. The wide receiver amassed more than 10,000 yards from 1968 to 1983. Today, he is the receivers' coach at Baylor University. He has appeared on *The Bernie Mack Show*.

The Rev. Jesse Jackson was a former quarterback for the University of Illinois and North Carolina A&T. He is now one of America's foremost civil rights activists and ran for the Democratic presidential nomination in 1984 and 1988. He is also the founder and president of the Rainbow/PUSH Coalition.

Roy S. Johnson is a writer and was an assistant managing editor at *Sports Illustrated* and a columnist for *The New York Times*.

Charlie Joiner played eighteen seasons in the NFL as a wide receiver and was an All Pro three times. He is a member of the Pro Football Hall of Fame.

Al Jury was an NFL official from 1978 to 2004. He was part of five Super Bowl officiating crews, including being the field judge in Super Bowl XXII.

Jack Kemp was a professional quarterback for eleven seasons and led the Buffalo Bills to two AFL championships in 1964 and 65. He spent eighteen years in the U.S. Congress and four years as Secretary of Housing and Urban Development under President George H.W. Bush. He ran for the Republican presidential nomination in 1988 and was the Republican Party's candidate for Vice President in 1996.

Norman H. Kimball spent nineteen years as general manager of the Edmonton Eskimos in the CFL and served as president and part owner of the Montreal Alouettes. In 1991, he was inducted into the Canadian Football Hall of Fame.

Frank Lewis was a number-one draft pick out of Grambling by the Pittsburgh Steelers in 1971. In thirteen NFL seasons, the wide receiver was elected to the Pro Bowl in 1981 while a member of the Buffalo Bills.

Floyd Little was a number-one draft pick by the Denver Broncos in 1967. In his nine seasons with the team, the running back rushed for over 6,000 yards and caught for more than 2,000 yards. He made the Pro Bowl five times.

Michael MacCambridge is the author of *America's Game: The Epic Story of How Pro Football Captured a Nation* and the editor of the *ESPN College*

Football Encyclopedia: The Complete History of College Football From 1869 to the Present.

Tom Mack played his entire thirteen-year career with the Los Angeles Rams. From 1966 to 1978, the offensive lineman earned eleven Pro Bowl invitations. He is a member of the Pro Football Hall of Fame.

Bob McElwee was an NFL official for twenty-seven years. He was the referee for three Super Bowls, including Super Bowl XXII.

Donovan McNabb is the quarterback for the Philadelphia Eagles. He was their number-one draft pick in 1999 and is a five-time All Pro.

Ron Meeks played with Arkansas State from 1972 to 1976 and in the CFL from 1977 to 1981. He has coached for several NFL teams and is currently the defensive coordinator for the Indianapolis Colts.

David Meggyesy was a linebacker for the St. Louis Cardinals and is the author of *Out of Their League*.

George Michael is a sportscaster and was the host of the long-running highlights show *The Sports Machine*.

Warren Moon quarterbacked the Washington Huskies to the Rose Bowl in 1978 and the CFL's Edmonton Eskimos to five championships. In his seventeen-year NFL career, he passed for 49,325 yards, the fourth most in history. He is a member of the Pro Football Hall of Fame and is one of the founders of the Field Generals.

Bill Nunn was a longtime editor at the *Pittsburgh Courier*. In 1969, he was hired by the Pittsburgh Steelers and their new coach, Chuck Noll, to be a full-time scout. He is still affiliated with the club.

Brigman Owens was an All-America quarterback at the University of Cincinnati and a safety for the Washington Redskins, from 1966 to 1977. After his football career, Owens went to law school and became the assistant executive director of the National Football League Players Association.

Vince Pisano was a high school and college teammate of Willie Thrower.

Brad Pye Jr. was a longtime sports editor of the *Los Angeles Sentinel* and a sports director at several radio stations.

John Rauch was the head coach of the Oakland Raiders from 1966 to 1968 and of the Buffalo Bills from 1969 to 1970. His record was 40–28–2.

Jimmy Raye was a standout quarterback for Michigan State from 1965 to 67 and led the Spartans to two Big Ten titles and the 1966 Rose Bowl. He was drafted by the Los Angeles Rams and switched to defensive back in the NFL. He began coaching in 1971, first in college and then for several NFL teams. He is currently the running backs coach for the New York Jets.

Jerry Rice was a wide receiver at Mississippi Valley State, which named its stadium for Rice and his quarterback, Willie Totten.

Rice played in the NFL for twenty seasons—most of them with the San Francisco 49ers—was the MVP in Super Bowl XXIII, and was a thirteen-time Pro Bowler. He is the all-time leading receiver in NFL history.

Ken Riley was a quarterback at Florida A&M and, from 1969 to 1983, a cornerback for the Cincinnati Bengals. Though he never made the Pro Bowl, he is fifth on the all-time interception list with sixty-five. He was also the head coach and athletic director at Florida A&M.

Charles Ross is an associate professor of history and African-American studies at the University of Mississippi and the author of *Outside the Lines: African-Americans and the Integration of the NFL.*

Andy Russell was a linebacker with the Pittsburgh Steelers for twelve seasons (1963, 1966 to 1976) and was elected to the Pro Bowl for seven of them.

Lou Saban coached in the AFL and NFL for sixteen seasons, between 1960 and 1976. In 1964 and 1965, he coached the Buffalo Bills to consecutive AFL championships. His cousin Nick Saban is the coach of the Miami Dolphins.

Eddie Sapir is a lawyer in New Orleans and Doug Williams' former agent.

Art Shell was an offensive lineman with the Oakland Raiders from 1968 to 1982 and a Pro Bowler for eight of those seasons. From 1989 to 1994, he coached the Raiders to a combined record of 54–38 and was named Coach of the Year for the 1990 season. In 2006, he began his second tour as the Raiders' coach, and he is a member of the Pro Football Hall of Fame.

Lovie Smith is the head coach of the Chicago Bears. He was the Associated Press Coach of the Year in 2005. He was also a coach at St. Louis and Tampa Bay.

Michael Smith is a senior writer for ESPN.com and a regular on ESPN's *Around the Horn*.

Stephen A. Smith was a sportswriter for the New York *Daily News* and *The Philadelphia Inquirer*. He has contributed to various TV and radio programs. He is now the host of ESPN's *Quite Frankly With Stephen A. Smith*.

Leigh Steinberg has been one of the sports world's leading agents since the 1970s. He is Warren Moon's agent.

George Taliaferro led the Indiana University offense as a single-wing tailback in the 1940s. He was an All-America in 1945, 47, and 48, and he led IU to an undefeated Big Ten title in 45. In 1949, he was the first African-American drafted by an NFL team, when the Chicago Bears selected him in the thirteenth round. In 1953, he became the first African-American to start at quarterback in an NFL game.

Willie Thrower was the first African-American quarterback to play in the Big Ten conference, helping Michigan State to a national championship in 1952. He was also the first African-American quarterback to complete a pass in the NFL.

Willie Thrower Jr. and Melvin Thrower are Willie Thrower's sons.

Steven Towns, one Fritz Pollard's grandsons, gave the acceptance speech when Pollard was inducted into the NFL Hall of Fame in 2005.

Gene Upshaw was an offensive lineman for the Oakland Raiders from 1967 to 1981. He was a Pro Bowler for seven of those seasons. He is the executive director of the NFL Players Association and a member of the Pro Football Hall of Fame.

Michael Vick is the quarterback for the Atlanta Falcons. He became the first African-American quarterback to be chosen with the first pick overall in the 2001 NFL draft.

Jay Walker, a former quarterback at Howard University, played briefly with the Patriots and Vikings. He is currently a state delegate in Maryland.

Seneca Wallace was a quarterback for Iowa State and is now playing with the Seattle Seahawks.

Paul Warfield was a wide receiver in the NFL from 1964 to 1977. He was a member of the 1972 Miami Dolphins team that finished undefeated and was an eight-time Pro Bowler. He is a member of the Pro Football Hall of Fame.

Murray Warmath was the head football coach at the University of Minnesota for eighteen seasons, from 1954 to 1971. He led the Gophers to a national championship in 1960, Big Ten championships in 1960 and 1967, and back-to-back Rose Bowl appearances in 1960 and 1961.

J.C. Watts was a quarterback at the University of Oklahoma and was the MVP of two Orange Bowl victories, in 1980 and 81. From 1981 to 1986, he played in the CFL for Ottawa. In 1994, he was elected to the U.S. Congress from the Fourth District of Oklahoma. In 2002, he retired from Congress and is now the chairman of the J.C. Watts Companies.

Dwight White was a defensive lineman for the Pittsburgh Steelers from 1971 to 1980. He was an All Pro in 1972 and 1973 and a member of four Super Bowl-winning teams. He is now a senior managing director of Mesirow Financial's public finance division.

Tom Wilkinson was a quarterback for Toronto, British Columbia, and Edmonton in the CFL. He is a member of the Canadian Football Hall of Fame.

Doug Williams was a quarterback at Grambling, finishing fourth in the 1977 Heisman voting, and led the Tampa Bay Buccaneers to the 1979 championship game. In 1988, he led the Washington Redskins to a Super Bowl victory, becoming the first African-American to do so. He was also voted MVP of that Super Bowl. From 1998 to

2003, he took over for retired legend Eddie Robinson as coach of Grambling, where he compiled a record of 52–18. Now a personnel executive with the Buccaneers, he is also one of the founders of the Field Generals.

Joe Gilliam and Terry Bradshaw, 1974.

CHAPTER ONE

JEFFERSON STREET JOE

*"I thought if you played well, you got to play. I guess I didn't under-
stand the significance of being a black quarterback at the time."*
—Joe Gilliam, Nashville Tennessean, 1999

J oe Gilliam was born in the limelight.
The son of a coach, he was schooled
in football from his first baby step. At
Tennessee State, the leonine six-foot-two, 187-pound quarterback dominated black
college football, throwing sixty-five touchdown passes in four seasons. His father,
Joe Gilliam Sr., ran the defense. The offense belonged to Joe Jr.

The younger Gilliam possessed excellent mechanics, counterbalanced by an
inspired spontaneity. He could execute set plays perfectly but was also capable of
creating big plays out of chaos and confusion. He was selected in the eleventh round
of the 1972 draft by the Pittsburgh Steelers, who already had two highly regarded,
highly drafted young quarterbacks: Terry Bradshaw and Terry Hanratty. Gilliam
stuck as the team's third-string, taxi-squad quarterback, thanks to his world-class

arm and, in some small measure, his craftiness. Concerned that the Steelers might do to him what NFL teams had done numerous times before to black quarterbacks—move him to wide receiver or defensive back—he intentionally ran slower in the forty-yard dash during training camp so that his speed couldn't be used as grounds for a switch.

In 1973, the year before the Steelers began their dynastic run of four world championships in six seasons, they were a very good football team with a very shaky sense of who their starting quarterback should be. Terry Bradshaw, the first player taken in the 1970 draft, opened the year as the starter but was roundly criticized, by fans and some members of the press, for lacking the necessary mental tools to lead the team. His backup, Terry Hanratty, was an unquestioned leader but couldn't come close to Bradshaw's physical prowess. And then there was the whiplike presence whose cannon arm produced perfect, feathery spirals. Gilliam made his professional debut on Monday Night Football in 1973, against the Washington Redskins. He took over in the third quarter for the injured Hanratty (Bradshaw was already hurt) and threw a forty-six-yard touchdown that helped the Steelers to a 21–16 victory.

Soon he was part of a simmering quarterback controversy, and as one of a scant few black quarterbacks in pro football, his race became a factor. Though Pittsburghers had embraced African-American stars for both the Pirates and the Steelers, the city was still a blue-collar town with pervasive prejudices. During his four seasons in Pittsburgh, Gilliam was the object of intense scrutiny and received virtually constant criticism from fans and the media—not to mention death threats and hate mail. The pressure and judgment hit him harder than it would most, leaving him suspicious of fans. As he explained once, most of the would-be friends and hangers-on "seem sincere, and all the time they're planning to fuck your mama and blow you up, too."

If Broadway Joe Namath was a revolutionary quarterback—a swaggering, flamboyant counterpart to the Johnny Unitas prototype—then Gilliam was a black Namath. The nickname Jefferson Street Joe, based on the name of the main street of black Nashville, perfectly suited the man who, for a brief time, would bear the brunt of the considerable expectations and prejudice that weighed on black quarterbacks.

Bill Nunn, longtime Steelers scout: Joe was accepted as a quarterback, but our thing going into that [1972] draft was that we already had quarterbacks. We had Bradshaw, we had Hanratty. We thought we were set. As a result, we really had Joey ranked much higher than he went. After a while, he was so high up on our board, we *had* to take him. I gave him a fourth-round rating because he was really thin, didn't have much weight, but everything else was there. And he had played against big-time competition. By the eleventh round, I said that the only thing preventing him from being accepted in the National Football League was him being black. That's when Chuck Noll said, "Let's take him."

Joe Greene, defensive lineman, two-time NFL Defensive Player of the Year: First thing I think when Joe Gilliam's name comes up is *tragic*. We saw what Joe could do with just a little bit of playing time [in 1972] his rookie year. During the strike season of 1974, he reported to camp and had a chance to work with rookies Lynn Swann and John Stallworth. That gave head coach Chuck Noll enough confidence to play him as a starter when things got a little shaky for Terry Bradshaw. And Joe did a good job. He did some things that

Terry could not, in terms of his pocket presence, his daringness, and completing passes downfield.

Joe Gilliam Sr.: Passing was Joey's game. That's how we won all those games at Tennessee State. He was ahead of Terry Bradshaw and Terry Hanratty when he got to the Steelers because they didn't come out of a history of passing.

Tony Dungy, University of Minnesota quarterback, former Steelers defensive back: Terry was more of a gunslinger, an easygoing guy, fun to be around. Joe was a professional quarterback coming out of college. He understood the game. He was accurate, he had a good arm, he was smart, and he loved to play.

Gene Upshaw, executive director, NFL Players Association: And what did Bradshaw think when he showed up at training camp and the Steelers had this black guy called Jefferson Street Joe out there throwing that goddamn ball to the other end of the field without even trying? I mean, bam, it's there! He had to think, Oh my God, this is what I'm up against.

Roy Blount Jr., author, *About Three Bricks Shy of a Load*: The first strong image I retain is of Joe Gilliam and Terry Bradshaw in Bradshaw's room, literally head-to-head, jocularly directing ethnic slurs at each other. I was pleased to see them uninhibited in that regard—they seemed to be quite friendly about those sorts of things.

I remember seeing Gilliam hanging from the goalposts, in a Y-shaped pose, hanging by his hands. It looked remarkably…like a crucifixion. He would hang that way to stretch himself out. He had lots of pain in his feet, and hanging like that must have taken some strain off them. But my main recollection is just how much fun it was to watch him play.

Joe Gilliam Sr.: One preseason in Latrobe, Pennsylvania, I was there with Joey. We go into the dining hall. Mean Joe Greene, L.C. Greenwood, and Ernie Holmes are sitting at a table by themselves. Joey comes in and sits at the table with the white guys. He had that kind of confidence. Bradshaw would not sit with the blacks. Hanratty would not sit with the blacks. Noll knew that Joey had leadership qualities because he had the confidence to handle any social situation. Bradshaw couldn't handle any kind of social situation.

Tony Dungy: It was Joe, Terry, and Terry. Kind of split three ways as to who should play. All the veterans said that Joe was the most talented guy—he had the best arm, and the best knowledge of the game. But Joe always felt that he had to be so much better to keep his job. He started the Super Bowl year because of the strike and developed that rapport with Swann and Stallworth. But it wasn't good enough just to win games. He felt like he had to win games throwing. Like he had to throw five touchdowns every week to keep his job. To a man, they'll tell you, in terms of talent and what the quarterback had to do—knowing the game, knowing the reads, and throwing the ball—Joe Gilliam had it all.

Roy Blount Jr.: I think it was hard during that time for quarterbacks who had played for predominantly African-American colleges to adapt to the NFL. To me, the way the game was played by those colleges was more exciting, but that wasn't what the pros were looking for. So there was a tension there. Steelers quarterbacks called their own plays, so a quarterback like Joe Gilliam, who liked to improvise and pass, pass, pass, was even more an element of uncertainty in the Steelers' system than he would have been in a system where the coach sent in the plays.

Joe Gilliam Sr.: Joey's IQ was up there in the 150s. He's like his mother: a very bright person. He knew what to do, knew how to be, knew what to say. We brought him up in private schools until he went to college. Because I was always on campus, you see. So Joey's education was better than most quarterbacks', particularly black quarterbacks'.

Frank Lewis, former Steelers wide receiver: Joe came from a school where all they did was put the ball in the air. He had a spear for an arm, but Pittsburgh just wasn't a passing team. Bradshaw was more of a hard-nosed guy who just played a solid, fundamental game. But Joe took over the position and very successfully led the team.

While most of the National Football League Players Association staged a strike during the 1974 preseason, Gilliam reported to camp intent on winning the quarterback job. He shined, while, later in the summer, a rusty Bradshaw seemed tentative. Before the Steelers' season-opening game against Baltimore, Noll announced that Gilliam would start at quarterback. With Gilliam under center, Pittsburgh won 30–0.

Dwight White, Steelers defensive lineman: Without taking away anything from Terry Bradshaw, he was really playing terrible. The strike may have had something to do with that, but I think it was more about performance. Joe was performing well, he was energetic, he made practices. In terms of the playbook, he did everything he was supposed to do. We were winning.

Rocky Bleier, former Steelers running back: When the season began, Joe was ready to go. He had decided to go to camp three weeks before the veterans, and those three weeks made a difference. For the first time in his life, Bradshaw had to sit on the bench behind another quarterback.

Joe Gilliam Sr.: You can't fault Noll. Bradshaw was slow upstairs. One time, I was in a meeting up there because I wanted to learn too, and [there's no better] teacher than Chuck Noll. He's trying to educate them on football, and there's Bradshaw with a little cup, and he's spitting tobacco juice in it and farting. It just infuriated Noll, but that's the kind of guy Bradshaw was. When it came to football smarts, he wasn't in the same class as Joey.

Rocky Bleier: Joe was a natural leader. He exuded confidence. He wasn't shy. He just took charge. And in that situation, that's all you're looking for: somebody to take charge and run things.

Andy Russell, former Steelers linebacker: He played so well in those [early-season] games. The one I remember well was in Denver. We tied 35–35. Our defense did not play well, but Joe played brilliantly. He dazzled all of us with his talent—his ability to feather the ball to a running back ten yards away or rocket it downfield to a wide receiver who was open for just a second. He was extraordinarily gifted. His ability to make decisions? I don't know. I don't mean to make the strike the reason he got the job. He was playing so well. I mean he was dazzling the coaches. He really had that kind of talent.

Joe Gilliam Sr.: At that time, Noll was both head coach and offensive coordinator. His entire offensive staff was vehemently against Joey being the quarterback, especially the receivers coach, Lionel Taylor, who was the leader of the group even though he was black. Taylor was a guy who really badly wanted to be white. He gave Joey living hell. But Chuck Noll said, "I think he's the better all-around quarterback, so I'm going to do it." And he did.

Frank Lewis: There wasn't any controversy in the locker room. We had three people who could play. If one goes down, somebody else is going to be able to come in and play. That's what made Pittsburgh so good during those years. We never lost a beat.

Andy Russell: We had tremendous rapport with all the guys—white guys, black guys—there was no color on the team. At least, that's the way it felt to me. I'd occasionally see a table [in camp] that was all black, and I'd go sit with them. Joe would do the opposite. I'd say we had zero problem with a black-white issue on those teams. On the field, it was, give all you have and do your job. Off the field, we were friends.

Though he showed occasional flashes, Gilliam suffered under the pressure and proved more inconsistent as the season went on. He completed just forty-five percent of his passes in '74, throwing four touchdown passes and eight interceptions, and also fumbling four times. Though Pittsburgh was 4–1–1, the offense wasn't performing as well as Chuck Noll had hoped.

Andy Russell: Noll never really wanted a wide-open passing attack. He was of the belief that when you pass the ball, three things can happen, and two of them are bad. So he wanted to have a running attack. Third and five, he'd give the ball to Franco Harris. His idea of a passing down was third and seven, third and eight. Gilliam was not doing what Chuck Noll wanted him to do, which was to give the ball to the running backs. He was checking off to passing plays. Bradshaw wanted to throw the ball too, but he handed it off.

Dwight White: We had the proverbial quarterback controversy. It got to the point where they actually put a ballot on the front page of the *Pittsburgh Post-Gazette*. A public opinion poll. The week after that, we went into the meeting room, and Chuck Noll says, "Bradshaw, you're up this week." Everybody was caught by surprise because we were winning. That's when the whole thing started—Joe's demise.

Rocky Bleier: If I'm not mistaken, Bradshaw got the nod to start in the Atlanta game. That was the beginning of the demise of Joe's self-esteem. My locker was right next to his. The question he asked of himself and the other players was, Why, why, why?

Joe Greene: If Bradshaw hadn't been a number one draft choice and we hadn't had some success with Terry, I think Noll would have let Joe go through that difficult stretch.

Joe Gilliam Sr.: Joey was never happy in the quarterback position. I remember one time my wife Ruth and I went to visit. The weather was cold up there. It was between games, during the week, and we were with him in his apartment. He said, "Come here, Daddy. Look in here." He opens the closet, and there's a huge cardboard box in there—must've been three by three—filled with letters to the very top. He said, "Read those letters, Daddy. Read some of them." I pick one up, and it's a death threat. I throw that one down. I pick up another one: a death threat. I said, "Joey, what's in here?" He said, "Dad, the whole box is full of death threats." I said, "I'm going to call Chuck Noll." He said, "No, Dad, he's on top of it. There's a guy down on the sidelines staking me out, because they say they're going to shoot me from the stands." None of his teammates would stand next to him.

Rocky Bleier: He showed me some of those letters. He'd go, "I don't believe this. I'm just trying to make the team."

Joe Greene: I couldn't walk in his shoes. I can't recall the fans in the city getting caught up in the controversy as much as the press, but from that time on, Joe self-destructed. Quite frankly, he was a coach's son who was a little bit spoiled.

Joe Gilliam Sr.: Coach Noll called me, and we talked it over for a long while. He said he had to take Joey out for the betterment of the team. And I agreed.

Frank Lewis: It's just like anything else. If you're going to work every day and you don't get that promotion you think you deserve, you start feeling different. But it's up to each individual [to determine] how you handle that, whether you let those down times depress you or you go on about your business. Joe just couldn't look past what was happening right then and there. We didn't have free agency. You were basically stuck with the team unless they cut you. If he could have just hung in there a little bit, I think things would have opened up. With his talent, there's no way in the world he could stay on the bench.

Bradshaw, whose statistics were equally unimpressive that season, has always praised his rival's talent, but he declined to be interviewed for this book. Though Gilliam won two Super Bowl rings as a backup with the Steelers, he found it difficult to share in the team's joy.

Marlin Briscoe, starting quarterback, Denver Broncos: When the Steelers used the Dolphins' training facility at Biscayne College to practice for Super Bowl X, Bradshaw and Hanratty took all the snaps. Gilliam was way off on the other field by himself, throwing at a goalpost. He had just exiled himself from the team. I went over and introduced myself and told him to hang in there. He was hurt and bitter. I guess he felt he wasn't part of the team anymore.

Andy Russell: I don't recall any disciplinary problems until Joe got benched. I was not that close to Joe—I was much older—but he seemed to be struggling. It was unheard of to be late to a meeting. We used to call it Lombardi time: Be at every meeting thirty minutes early. When Joe had been late a few times, you start to think, Something's going on here. What's he doing? He seemed to deteriorate. During a Saturday night game against the Rams in '75, center Ray Mansfield told me Joe was out of control in the huddle. I don't know how to describe it, as though he was a bit delirious, not making sense, just winging the ball carelessly. It didn't seem like he was ready to play. It wasn't a critical game. We could've lost and still made the playoffs. He approached it almost like an exhibition game. He did badly. As I recall, he threw a number of interceptions. Really imploded. Whether that was a result of the pressure and the disappointment, or of him finding solace in a bottle or a pill—whatever, he just seemed to be going downhill. I heard rumors that he was doing drugs, but I have no verification.

Ernie Holmes, former Steelers defensive lineman: He'd been into marijuana. After the job got transferred back to Terry, that's when the drug use escalated. It went from coke to speed to heroin, he was experimenting with everything. Receiver Rod Shanklin, myself, Joe Greene, defensive end L.C. Greenwood, all of us tried to talk with him. He would go off into this little pantomime of Richard Pryor. Joe was kind of a comedian. He used to go, "Nigga, nigga, nigga, nigga, nigga," getting all up in everybody's face in a rebellious response to the way he was being handled.

Bill Nunn: Different things went on. I don't need to go into that. Because I could go into that with other guys, too. White guys, too.

Roy Blount Jr.: I don't think the Steelers knew what he was doing drugwise, but it was certainly more than anybody else was doing. It got beyond the pale, beyond what anyone else on the team would understand. A lot of the black players felt he'd let them down.

Ernie Holmes: He was extremely depressed about losing the starting position. We tried to get him to calm down, but he started going through a lot of things to express his anger. Every now and then, you'd see guys do a little coke, a little weed. One time, Joey really went off the deep end. He was my roommate on the road. We were playing the Raiders up in Oakland. That night he came in late. I told him he ought to get himself together. He stayed there awhile. He had a girlfriend with him. Then he went back out. It was way after curfew, but he went out anyway. He didn't return until about thirty minutes before we went on the field for the warm-ups. He had coke with him when he came into the locker room, in one of those aluminum foil things. I snatched it from him and went straight to the commode and flushed it. He got kinda pissed off, but I told him, "What the hell you think you're doing? You're really pissing me off. You're disrespecting me. You're disrespecting all of us. I don't know what the hell is wrong with you. If you got a problem with the quarterback change, hell, take it up with Chuck. Because right now, you're kicking all our asses." He just dropped his head and started that Richard Pryor stuff again.

Gene Upshaw: He just drifted off. Got into drugs, got into the fast lane, and wasn't able to get out. When I saw he had passed away at 49, it didn't surprise me. He was always on the edge like that.

Michael MacCambridge, author, *America's Game: The Epic Story of How Pro Football Captured a Nation:* In retrospect, it's striking to think how close Gilliam might have come to running that great Steelers team, and being at the center of that dynasty. I've spoken to many football people who feel that if he hadn't been black, he would have received a longer look at the beginning of the '74 season. I disagree—the people who played for him say Noll was color-blind. I think it's likely that any quarterback having Joe's problems moving the offense might have been lifted on a team in which the alternatives were so attractive. You certainly can't criticize Noll based on the career that Bradshaw enjoyed and the four Super Bowl rings he won. But it's also true that the burden of being one of the first black quarterbacks in the limelight left an indelible mark on Gilliam. It didn't merely affect his game, it affected his life.

Gilliam signed with the Saints in 1976 and was cut shortly thereafter for disciplinary reasons. Gilliam could not beat his demons. Even a 1983 attempt to revive his career with the USFL's Washington Federals failed. He was homeless for a little while and pawned his Super Bowl rings to pay for drugs, but he recovered with the help of his father.

Joe Gilliam Sr.: He did that thing you can't do: drugs. That was the reality of it, and I'm troubled every day of my life because of it. Every day. I think I might have put too much time into football and not enough time into the kid. That's a real possibility if you know the way I went after football. Maybe I came up short there. You can't place all the blame on the kid. One time, Ruth and I were out with Howard Gentry, who was the athletic director at Tennessee State, and his wife, Carrie. Their son and Joey grew up together. I'm walking across a parking lot with Carrie Gentry, and she asks me how Joey's doing. I said, "Carrie, he's not doing worth a damn." We got to talking about it, and she said, "Joe, I can tell from the way you're saying things that you're on the wrong track." I said, "What do you mean?" She said, "That's your child. What you have not extended to him is unconditional love." I said, "Unconditional?" I'm supposed to be an educated man. Hell, I'm teaching graduate school. This is escaping me. I said, "What are you talking about? I love my son." She said, "Look, unconditional love means you love him when he's good and you love him when he's bad." I said, "Well, I fall out with him when he's bad." In other words, when he's doing drugs. She said, "How can you expect anyone in the community to extend him unconditional love when his daddy, who is responsible for him being here, does not extend that love to him?" That shook me up. From that day in 1979 until this day, I've made certain that I gave all kids hell when they were wrong, but I tried to end it with a hug and a kiss. You have to do it. You have to give them hell, but you have to hug them. You have to.

Baltimore Colts quarterback Johnny Unitas, 1971.

CHAPTER TWO

"EYES ARE ON YOU"

I n the years following World War II, the halfback-led single wing steadily gave way to the T formation as the offense of choice in pro football. As a result, the quarterback quickly became the most important figure on the field. In the T, he was both catalyst and focal point, a leader who needed more than mere physical skills. He had to be nimble, able to take the snap from under center, and distribute the ball to his running backs. He had to be a gifted passer, able to throw the ball to his receivers under pressure. And it helped if he was somewhat elusive, to avoid the rush that was becoming an integral part of the game. He was, in essence, a coach on the field, the guy who understood the playbook as well as the team's offensive philosophy. He needed to be wily, in order to read opposing defenses and adjust his playcalling accordingly. Above all, he had to be a "leader of men."

That last part was more subjective, and it became a source of controversy whenever the relative merits of great quarterbacks were being discussed. The Cleveland Browns began play in 1946 and, using the T, went to ten title games in their *first ten seasons—winning seven—but their quarterback, Otto Graham, was diminished in some people's eyes because he wasn't calling his own plays.*

With the arrival of John Unitas to the Baltimore Colts in 1956, the die was cast for all future players at that position. Unitas, shoe-leather tough and unflappable, possessed a pointed coolness, a sense of reserve with which he separated himself from (and lifted himself slightly above) his teammates. In pro football, Unitas' influence was vast. The ineffable qualities that made Unitas respected by his teammates became the working definition of "the right stuff" and were inextricably bound up in future discussions of which qualities a quarterback ought to possess. Any quarterback who veered from this script— scramblers like Fran Tarkenton, long-throwers like Daryle Lamonica—were subject to criticism.

Into this rigid context stepped the first professional black quarterbacks, in the late sixties. To have an African-American take the position of responsibility—at a time when the nation was still polarized over basic questions of civil rights—was not merely a departure, it was a subversion of much of the conventional wisdom of postwar America.

Some of the country was ready for the change. Many pro football coaches and owners clearly were not.

Charles Ross, author, *OTL: African-Americans and the Integration of the NFL*: The quarterback is a team's general. He leads an offense the way a general leads an army. He's there to direct the battle. In a society in which white men have always dominated positions of power, it's hardly surprising to see African-Americans barred from the leadership role on the football field. To see African-Americans assume this particular position speaks volumes about how people look at an individual and a team.

Tony Dungy: It's hard for people in this day and age to understand how much the quarterback was looked to as the leader. Until Tom Landry came into pro football, the quarterback was more in charge than the head coach. The quarterback called the plays. He orchestrated the whole game. Putting that control in one person's hands made the quarterback an icon, more so than the point guard in basketball or the catcher or pitcher in baseball. It isn't an unspoken rule, either. It's clearly stated that this guy's in charge of the team.

Chuck Ealey, former starting quarterback in the CFL and at the University of Toledo: If you look at the things that were happening to black people in the early fifties and early sixties—in the wake of Jackie Robinson—all the progress was based on society feeling freer. But the perception among NFL ownership, as silly as it was, was that a black quarterback couldn't perform at the leadership position. When I was growing up, I didn't have a black quarterback to emulate. The only quarterbacks I saw were white—Fran Tarkenton or Y.A. Tittle.

Tony Dungy: It wasn't like there were no black quarterbacks; Sandy Stephens led Minnesota to the national championship in 1960. But once you got to the pros, they weren't willing to put a black man in control.

Stephen A. Smith, host, ESPN's *Quite Frankly With Stephen A. Smith*: The fact is, you had a lot of people who questioned the intellectual capacity of the black quarterback. His ability to lead. The willingness of others to follow him. All those things came into play.

The perception was that the black athlete was inferior intellectually. And we all know that in the game of football, you have to be an intellectual to play the quarterback position.

Starting with Iowa's Wilburn Hollis, Minnesota's Sandy Stephens, and Michigan State's Jimmy Raye coming out of the Big Ten in the Sixties, many black quarterbacks who'd succeeded in college football never got a chance to prove themselves in the pros. Chuck Ealey won thirty-five consecutive games at Toledo from 1969 to 1971 but never got a shot to quarterback in the NFL. For Ealey and other black quarterbacks, the land of opportunity was Canada, where the three-down system offered a wide-open game, and racial attitudes were less onerous.

Tony Dungy: Chuck Ealey was the star of the Mid-American Conference in the early Seventies. Chuck Ealey was my hero. Toledo won, like, thirty-five straight games. If you win that many games, you'd think you'd get an opportunity in the NFL. He didn't. He went to Canada and won the Grey Cup his first year. Chuck was the ultimate winner, but he never got the chance to win in the NFL.

Chuck Ealey: I could have gotten drafted, but I made it pretty clear [to pro scouts] I wanted to go as a quarterback. Based on my winning record, I expected to have the opportunity. But when I didn't get it, I moved on. I was disappointed, but it wasn't earth-shattering. I can't say every team in the NFL refused to draft me because I was black. I can't say every team required me to be six-two and 220 pounds. But every team in the NFL wanted someone who can lead and be a winner. I went through three years of university football on teams that didn't lose a game. Didn't I at least deserve a try?

Wilburn Hollis, former quarterback, University of Iowa: I felt it when I was trying out for professional football. You had to be two times better than whites—four times better if you were trying to be a quarterback. There was just no way you were going to walk into an NFL camp and be a black quarterback unless you were three or four times better than what you were facing.

Danny Barrett, former starting quarterback in the CFL and at the University of Cincinnati: If you were a black quarterback [in the Seventies], you were almost always moved to another position. There was no rationale. They didn't want to give you the benefit of the doubt. In baseball, Branch Rickey was willing to step up and allow Jackie Robinson to cross the barrier. The Dodgers took a chance. It wasn't until the late Eighties that you started to see people give black quarterbacks an opportunity. Before that, it took bold men to step up and say, Hey, I'm going to give James Harris or Doug Williams an opportunity to play the position. Someone had to step out and give those guys a shot.

Tony Dungy: The scouts said I wasn't good enough to play quarterback [in the pros], so I ended up going to Pittsburgh and switching positions. I played on defense. As I watched the guys who were playing quarterback, I saw a lot who weren't very good. It took me about a year to come to the conclusion that I could have played quarterback.

Brigman Owens, former quarterback, University of Cincinnati: I remember Tom Landry telling me he wanted me to try defensive back. I said I'd never played the position before, never even tackled anyone. He said "You're a great athlete, and we need to find a place for you on this team." The very first tackle I ever made, I wound up with eleven stitches over my eye. We were doing nutcracker drills, and Amos Marsh was the running back. He had thighs as big as my body. I was thinking, I've got to get him before he gets any speed. I hit him real good, got his feet off the ground. What I thought was sweat coming down my forehead was blood.

Danny Barrett: I signed with the CFL prior to the NFL draft—1983, the Year of the Quarterback. I wasn't surprised that I didn't get a call from the NFL, but I was surprised I didn't get one from the USFL. My numbers were just as good as the other guys coming out. Reggie Collier, a black quarterback from Southern Miss, also came out that year. And Homer Jordan, who won a national championship at Clemson. And Steve Clarkson, who played out west at San Jose State. Only one of us had an opportunity to play in the postseason games: the East-West, Blue-Gray, or Hula Bowl. We weren't getting invited to those games. So you know something wasn't right.

Brigman Owens: During my first two weeks in Washington, Otto Graham walked up to me and said, "Don't get any bright ideas. As long as I'm coach, you're never playing quarterback." Back then, the NFL champions played the college all-stars each year. When I was at Cincinnati, Graham had coached the college team. He said, "When I coached the all-star game, your name came up, and I'm the one who struck it down because I didn't want a black quarterback on my college team." I said, "You gotta be kidding me."

Bill Curry, ESPN analyst and former All-Pro NFL center: In the world we grew up in, the people who held the keys to the tower were elderly white people. The lightning rods, the leaders, were chosen based on the fact that they resembled those in power. You could just sense it. In the early Seventies, we had an African-American quarterback in Baltimore named Carl Douglas. He had enormous talent, but you sensed somehow that he was not going to be the starting quarterback. Certain organizations made fundamental decisions that were very, very obvious. There weren't many African-American players on the New York Yankees for a long time. There weren't many African-American players on the Packers. But as you dig, it's going to be hard to find people who will blurt out the truth because it's still such a political flash point. To this very day, people are reluctant to say, "Oh yeah, this organization was just not going to have an African-American quarterback."

Michael MacCambridge: Even as pro football resisted the change, you could see the way it was affecting college football, even in the Deep South. Condredge Holloway became something of a folk hero down in Tennessee, leading the Volunteers to three bowl games in the early Seventies. In the early Eighties, Turner Gill, the first black starting quarterback at Nebraska, was the centerpiece of a devastating offense: Heisman winner Mike Rozier, wingback Irving Fryar, a truly great offensive line. Rozier won the awards, Fryar went first in the NFL draft, but Gill was the preeminent figure on the team, just a beloved player in Nebraska. He had that mystique of leadership that all great quarterbacks possess. To see the effect that Gill had on Huskers fans during that period was to see people's attitudes changing right before your eyes. But he wasn't a traditional, six-foot-three dropback quarterback, so he didn't get a chance in the NFL.

The first African-American quarterbacks to play during the era of widespread media coverage—Marlin Briscoe in Denver in the late Sixties, James Harris in Buffalo and Los Angeles, and Joe Gilliam in Pittsburgh in the early Seventies—ran up against unfair questions concerning their ability to lead, as well as resistance to the smallest deviation from the classic dropback quarterback mold. On top of all that came the pressure that accompanies the most-scrutinized position in the world of sports.

Randall Cunningham, former Pro Bowl quarterback: Everybody thinks it's all glitz and glamour, but people don't realize the pressure that's on a quarterback. When you go up to the line of scrimmage, you've got everybody's position and the various motions running through your mind. Couple that with a 350-pound guy coming at you from the blind side while you're dropping back, and fans spitting in your face and cursing you and your family out. If you can't thrive under that pressure, you will never be successful.

Condredge Holloway, first black SEC quarterback: Even when you hand the ball off, there's somebody watching you. If you stop, they double-team somebody else. But if you carry out a fake or go back like you're going to pass, you can take a man away. Somebody's always watching you.

Doug Williams, MVP, Super Bowl XXII: You take a step, eyes are on you. You drop back, eyes are on you. You lift your arm, eyes are on you.

Michael Smith, senior writer, ESPN.com: Quarterback is the toughest job in all of sports, no question about it. The game starts with the quarterback and ends with the quarterback. It's not the same as pitching in baseball, not the same as point guard in basketball. It's all on you. Even marginal quarterbacks have an exceptional amount of responsibility.

Bill Curry: The quarterback has to have an intuitive feel for what's happening. He's got to have what's called second sight, meaning he can sense things other people can't. It's a mystical kind of thing. All great quarterbacks have it.

Joe Greene: Terry Bradshaw really put it in perspective. He said, "You can lose with me, but you can't win without me." That's the deal with the quarterback. You can get angry with them because they do many bad things with the ball, but they also do many good things. Every time the ball is snapped, they've got it.

J.C. Watts, former U.S. congressman and former quarterback, University of Oklahoma: You're the offensive coordinator, psychiatrist, motivator, passer, runner, you've got to do it all. I don't care how good the roster is, the success of the team is determined by the quarterback. And that becomes more of a factor the higher up you go.

Stephen A. Smith: You can only go as far as your quarterback takes you. He's the field general, the first line of communication with the coach. Without him, things don't get executed. Everybody follows his lead. When you don't respect your quarterback, your offense is in trouble. Your whole team is in trouble.

Bill Curry: Great quarterbacks have an element of can-do, whether it's Bart Starr, Johnny Unitas, or Earl Morrall—the guys I was lucky to play with. It's a leadership presence, military bearing—the kind of stuff George Patton had.

Condredge Holloway: You have to have an arrogance about you, but in a way that's not offensive or cocky. When you call out a play in the huddle, they've got to believe that you believe that play will work. That only happens if they've got confidence in you. They don't have to like you. They don't have to be your best buddies. But they've got to believe in you. Once they do, you've all got one heartbeat.

Doug Williams: You're talking about a position that was reserved for the white man. Control, brains, and the ability to lead are things that, historically, blacks are not supposed to have. Grambling coach Eddie Robinson used to tell us that every man is born equal to become unequal.

J.C. Watts: I think corporate America—and when I say corporate America, I include the National Football League's owners and operators—has always had a difficult time taking judgment from black men. You probably can count on one hand the number of starting black quarterbacks. You can count on the other hand the number of black offensive or defensive coordinators. Even at the college and high school level, it's always been a challenge.

Todd Boyd, professor of critical studies, University of Southern California: In unspoken ways, the quarterback was thought to look a certain way, to speak a certain way, to act a certain way, to embrace certain political ideas. He was the quintessential white man. For a lot of people, putting a black person in that position was something they simply couldn't resolve to do.

Jerry Rice, MVP, Super Bowl XXIII: It has a lot to do with image. There was this perception that the quarterback had to be smart. There are a lot of black individuals—including black quarterbacks—who are very smart, but it took awhile for people to realize that.

The Rev. Jesse Jackson, civil rights activist and former quarterback, University of Illinois and North Carolina A&T: People saw Jerry Rice at Mississippi Valley State, but they did not see his quarterback, Willie Totten. All those balls Jerry Rice caught? A guy named Willie Totten threw them.

Todd Boyd: For a lot of people, to have a black man in this position of leadership was inconsistent with the way they saw black people in society. It was assumed that black players could do certain things on the field, but lead the team, lead a group of men, was not one of them—because you didn't have prominent black leaders in other positions of authority in society. Football was simply a reflection of that.

Danny Barrett: They always say the black quarterback is athletic. But the bottom line is you have to have the ability to make plays. That's all the personnel guys look at. Whether it's with your arm or your legs, can you make plays and give them an opportunity to win more games.

Roy S. Johnson, former assistant managing editor, *Sports Illustrated*:
Think about the quarterback in history. Not just on the field, but in society. He's the guy who gets the prettiest girl at the high school prom, he's the student-body president. The quarterback is the glamour guy. When a team wins, the quarterback gets the credit. He gets elevated to this position of idolatry. Because of all that, because of the people who represented that position—from Johnny Unitas to Joe Namath—it was very hard for society in general and the NFL specifically to embrace the idea that a black man could be that type of idol.

Kevin Carroll, motivational speaker and former NBA trainer, Philadelphia 76ers: When football integrated, it gave black athletes roles to play. They were not to be the focal point of the team. The quarterback was the last bastion of white supremacy. The quarterback has always stepped onto the field as the leader, since the days of the old, grainy footage. The guy doing the voice-over emphasized the quarterback. It was branding before people even knew the term. They were creating a way for people to affiliate with the team—through Johnny Unitas, Bart Starr, Sonny Jurgensen, Y.A. Tittle, Joe Namath. For black quarterbacks, it was like, How do we market Doug Williams? How do we market Warren Moon? That's not our target customer.

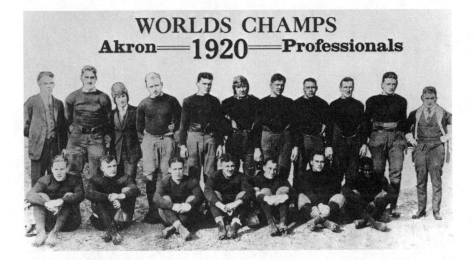

Fritz Pollard (bottom right) and the Akron Professionals, 1920.

CHAPTER THREE

PIONEERS

The struggle to level the playing field at quarterback dates back to the game's formative years, when Frederick "Fritz" Pollard, a brash young halfback who led Brown to the Rose Bowl in 1915, emerged as one of pro football's first stars, guiding the Akron Pros to a championship in the 1921 season. One year later, he took charge of the team, becoming the game's first African-American coach. More than a shining light, Pollard exemplified the courage and determination needed to succeed in a truly hostile arena.

Jerry Izenberg, sportswriter, *Newark Star-Ledger:* When Fritz Pollard arrived on campus, there were only two blacks; one was the custodian, he was the other. His only friends were on the football team. Quarterback meant nothing to him. It was all about making the football team at Brown. He made that very clear. He wasn't trying to break the color line. He wanted to go to that school, so he went. He was amazed they let him do it. Really amazed.

Steven Towns, Fritz Pollard's grandson: At the time, there were only about fifty African-Americans attending college in the whole country—three or four were Pollards.

Charles Ross: You had a left halfback, a right halfback, and then the quarterback. The quarterback barked out the signals, but the ball was snapped directly to the left halfback, who was, for all practical purposes, your best running back. He could run or throw the football or toss it to the right halfback or the quarterback. Pollard was a left halfback, but he had the opportunity to play this position of quarterback in several games as well.

Steven Towns: The chants started at a game at Yale. The crowd sang "Bye, Bye Black Bird" while he was on the field. If you look at the last interview he did before he passed away, he had tears in his eyes when reliving that moment.

He didn't graduate from Brown. He was deemed academically ineligible. In his home, education was key, but once he got out, he ran a little wild. He didn't go to class. He wound up in Pennsylvania, helping his brother Luther coach at Lincoln University. Frank Neid, who owned the Akron Pros, called him up and asked him to play. He played offense and defense, did all the kickoffs, the punting, and the field goals. He returned kicks, too. He never left the field.

Jerry Izenberg: When he got to Akron, Pollard was not allowed to dress in the locker room. He had to dress in this boarding house, then walk down the street in his uniform. In those days, you didn't go into the locker room at halftime—you sat on the ground and talked—so he never really got into the locker room. Not until a year later, when they fired the coach and decided to make him coach. Outside of the black schools, Fritz Pollard was the first black to be a head coach in any sport in America. Baseball didn't even have black players. The Akron Pros won seven straight games his first year as a head coach [all of them shutouts]. Then they went bad and fired him, and he was back to changing in the boarding house again.

Steven Towns: He had to roll on his back with his cleats up after he got tackled to protect himself from the piling-on. He remembered being chased into the stands by opposing players. He'd run out of bounds and they kept after him. He had to be escorted onto the field because the crowd would throw things at him. He couldn't eat with the team. Because of the times, there wasn't a whole lot he could do. He just had to put up with it.

Charles Ross: People tend to focus on baseball. At the time of Jackie Robinson's breakthrough, it was the dominant team sport in the United States. What's often forgotten is that African-Americans played in the National Football League from the time of its creation in the 1920s. For a decade or so, they played on various teams. But after the 1933 season, a color barrier was instituted. It lasted until 1946. Players such as Fritz Pollard argued that black players were used as pawns to attract fans, until the franchise owners developed a stable fan base. There's probably some merit to that argument.

In 1939, Kenny Washington was the best college player in the United States. He was a quadruple threat from the left halfback position. He could throw, he could run, he could catch, and he could kick. His UCLA team went undefeated. He wasn't drafted. In 1941, Jackie Robinson was an outstanding halfback at UCLA, the star of the annual all-star game between the best college players and the NFL champions. He wasn't drafted. In 1945, Bill Willis of Ohio State was a consensus choice as the best offensive lineman in the country. He wasn't drafted. On and on and on. It wasn't like baseball, where owners could argue—however disingenuously—that they had no way to know if black players could play at the Major League level. Pro football owners watched black players like Jackie Robinson compete against their league champions in all-star games every year. They obviously preferred *not* to see.

According to a story in the *Chicago Defender*, a black newspaper, George Halas told Kenny Washington after he played in the 1940 all-star game, "Wait around. Don't leave Chicago." The speculation is that Halas went to the NFL's other owners and tried to talk them into letting the Bears draft Washington. He came back and, in essence, told Washington, "I can't use you. It's not going to work out." Washington ended up playing for the Hollywood Bears, a semi-pro team in L.A. He did all right, making a bit more money than the average NFL player because he was paid a percentage of the gate.

Michael MacCambridge: The Cleveland Rams won the NFL title in 1945 and announced a month later that they were moving to Los Angeles. The move was approved by the NFL on January 11, 1946. Three days later, a city commission met in L.A. to determine if the team could play in the Coliseum. Before the meeting, three journalists for African-American newspapers—Halley Harding of the *Los Angeles Tribune* and Herman Hill and J.C. Fentress of the *Pittsburgh Courier*—

asked the chairman of the commission, Leonard Roach, for a chance to speak. Harding spoke at length and with eloquence, decrying the color line in pro football. He called it "singularly strange" that Kenny Washington had never been offered an NFL contract. Rams' GM Chile Walsh vowed then and there that Washington would be offered a tryout. That's how pro football was reintegrated—months before Jackie Robinson broke the color line in baseball.

Charles Ross: The United States had just fought a world war to defend freedom and democracy all across the world. How could you deny those basic rights to African-Americans? Washington got his shot—albeit too late. He was no longer as sharp as he had been in 1939 when he graduated from UCLA. Woody Strode was brought in that same year, mostly to give Washington someone to room with.

In Cleveland, the Browns deserve credit for simply doing the right thing. Paul Brown, a former head coach at Ohio State and the Great Lakes Naval Station, was a part owner of the new Cleveland entry in the All-America Football Conference. He decided in August of '46 to invite Bill Willis, an African-American defensive lineman who had played for him at Ohio State, to camp. Brown didn't let the other players know what he was up to. Willis just showed up on his way to Canada, presumably to play Canadian football. He simply suited up and started going to practice. Brown figured correctly that Willis' achievements on the practice field would verify for the players that he could play.

The next step was easy. Signing fullback Marion Motley, like the signing of Woody Strode by the Rams, was motivated by the need to have someone for Willis to room with on the road. Putting a white player in with a black player wasn't going to happen. Neither was eating the cost of a private room.

Willis and Motley became integral parts of the Browns, got a lot of support from local fans, helped Cleveland win championships in the AAC and the NFL, and capped their great careers by being inducted into the Pro Football Hall of Fame.

Though players were quick to see the merits of signing talented black athletes, the men who controlled the rosters were far less receptive to the idea. Their resistance was plain to see from 1933 to 1946, but they were careful not to express their opinions in public. All, that is, except one very vocal, very strong-willed man.

Charles Ross: George Preston Marshall, owner of the Washington Redskins, headed the group of owners who were hostile to integration. His position was pretty much summed up by something he once said: "We're going to play black players when the Harlem Globetrotters have white players."

Tom Friend, Senior Writer, *ESPN The Magazine*: George Preston Marshall was notorious—the most racist owner of all time. In that era, each team had their own television network and Redskins games were televised throughout the South. They had the whole region to themselves. To this day, if the Redskins play in Carolina or Atlanta, you'll see lots of Redskins fans.

Charles Ross: The Redskins were eventually integrated in 1962, but only after considerable pressure from the Kennedy Administration, namely Secretary of the Interior Stewart Udall. As in Los Angeles, the message from Udall to Marshall was simple: "If you want to play in D.C. Stadium, a public facility built with tax dollars, you have to bring in black players." Marshall relented and traded the draft rights of Ernie Davis to the Cleveland Browns for Bobby Mitchell.

Tom Friend: Shirley Povich, a legendary *Washington Post* columnist, once wrote this great lead, poking fun at Marshall's absurd stance. The Redskins had just played the Cleveland Browns. "Jim Brown, born ineligible to play for the Redskins, integrated their end zone three times yesterday" [in a 31–10 victory]. That's still one of the greatest lines ever.

To overcome the prejudice in the professional leagues, African-Americans had to win the hearts of the coaches in the college ranks—no easy task, especially in the football strongholds of the South. Syracuse stood at the vanguard in the East, riding the remarkable play of Wilmeth Sidat-Singh—whom the immortal sportswriter Grantland Rice canonized alongside other passing greats Sid Luckman and Sammy Baugh—to a 1938 upset of a very good Cornell team. USC and UCLA were the gateways to opportunity in the West. But the Big Ten conference tossed out the biggest welcome mat. Between 1945 and 1975, no less than a dozen African-American signal callers dotted the campuses of middle America. Among them were Willie Thrower, Jimmy Raye, and Tyrone Willingham of Michigan State, Wilburn Hollis of Iowa, and Sandy Stephens and Tony Dungy of Minnesota. Even a young man named Jesse Jackson spent his freshman season under center at Illinois.

George Taliaferro, halfback, Indiana University: Joe Gilliam Sr. was the first black quarterback in the conference. He played in a game in November 1945, when Indiana beat Minnesota 49–0 and I scored the first three touchdowns. Indiana had four black people in the backfield at the same time. Joe was the quarterback, Jackie Adams was left halfback, Bill Bradley was right halfback, and Bill Buckner, Quinn Buckner's father, was fullback.

Marlin Briscoe: I remember watching Sandy Stephens and Wilburn Hollis play in the Big Ten. There was a little grassy knoll, a triangle, in front of the project where I lived. I used to go out there and pretend I was Johnny Unitas—because there were no black quarterbacks in the pros. But in 1960, I pretended to be Sandy Stephens of Minnesota and Wilburn Hollis of Iowa. Wilburn was from Omaha, my hometown. He was dating a girl named Shirley Higgins, who had been my babysitter. One day, I was shooting marbles in the backyard and who walks up but Wilburn Hollis. He had his Iowa jacket on and I was like—I couldn't believe it. Here he was in the flesh!

Jimmy Raye, quarterback, Michigan State: No question who my role model was: Sandy Stephens. I sing his praises whenever I can, because without Sandy Stephens, there would have been no me. He gave me hope—the will to go forward.

When they used to introduce the team on TV, you'd run up in front of the camera and pronounce your name, then run out: "Sandy Stephens, quarterback, Uniontown, P.A. Boom!" Up until that point, I was going to Florida A&M, Tennessee State, Morgan, North Carolina A&T, or North Carolina Central. Those were the choices you had in the South because you couldn't go to the Atlantic Coast conference.

It was against the law to give a black athlete a scholarship. But when I saw Sandy play, I knew I could go to the Big Ten.

Wilburn Hollis: Big Ten coaches signed black quarterbacks because they wanted winners. Pretty soon other coaches were saying, "Whoa! If we have black quarterbacks who are good, knowledgeable, intelligent people, why can't we win with them?"

Tony Dungy: I went to Minnesota because they had a history of black quarterbacks. I knew race was not going to be an issue. Most of the guys who went into the Big Ten felt that way. I remember Dennis Green saying that's why he went to Iowa. He watched Minnesota playing Iowa in the Game of the Week. One team was Number One, the other was Number Three, and they both had black quarterbacks. He was so fired up about that, he knew he wanted to go to a Big Ten school.

Willie Thrower was the star halfback at New Kensington High in western Pennsylvania when a Michigan State coach came knocking on his door. Thrower's talent was so pronounced that he had been invited to play in a 1948 all-star game in Texas—as captain of the East team. But when the game's organizers discovered he was black, he was told he could not take the field. MSU's line coach, Duffy Daugherty, a former Syracuse teammate of Wilmeth Sidat-Singh, had no such hang-ups. Neither did his boss, the legendary Spartan coach Clarence "Biggie" Munn. They both recognized Thrower's phenomenal arm strength and quickly converted him to quarterback, where he backed up All-American Tom Yewcic on the 1952 national championship team.

Willie Thrower*: I played halfback in high school. My great friend Cubby France was the quarterback. The offense was really geared toward me from the halfback spot. We had a multiple offense—single wing, wing T, and straight T. In the single wing, the ball would come straight back to me and I would either hold it, hand it to the fullback or halfback, or fade back and pass.

Melvin Thrower, Willie Thrower's son: He won the state championship in '46 and '47. They had to enlarge the stadium because they were drawing so many people to the games. It only held about 5,500. There were people standing in the aisles, standing in the road. They had to enlarge the stadium so it would hold about 10,000 people.

Willie Thrower: We lost the championship game when I was a freshman. We lost to Dinaro. They beat us pretty bad, 38–6. We had all freshman and sophomores on that team. Most of them ended up going to Michigan State. Duffy Daugherty took eight of us. Later on, the Michigan legislature put it on the record that Michigan State would never take eight boys from one school again because we've got kids from this state who want to play, too. But we got them a championship in 1952.

Every college in the country wanted me—schools like Miami, Georgia, Kentucky—but as soon as they saw I was black, that was the end of it. So I went north to Michigan State, where we had a fellow in front of me named Al Dorow who later went to the Washington Redskins. Our stadium held 50,000 fans and they would chant, "We want Willie! We want Willie!"

* Willie Thrower's comments are excerpted from an audio interview conducted before he passed away. The full interview can be heard on williethepro.com.

Melvin Thrower: He told me he could throw the ball about eighty yards. People around here say he could throw it longer than that—ninety yards, a hundred yards. Michigan State is up near Lake Erie. It was real windy up there. One day, the coach said, "Willie, get in there! Get in there!" He told him to get on the field and throw the ball from the forty-yard line. That's how they practiced kickoff returns. So he lined up on the forty and threw the ball all the way downfield.

Willie Thrower: I was a quarterback from the time I went there until the time I left. I didn't play as much ball as I should have, and the fans knew it. It was amazing what they did for me.

Vince Pisano, high school and college teammate of Willie Thrower: If we were ahead, they'd put him in and he'd call all pass plays. The whole student body would holler, "We want Willie!"

Melvin Thrower: He was in "Ripley's Believe It or Not" for the most famous hand, because his hand was so large. You couldn't even see the ball when his hand was over it.

Willie Thrower Jr.: We used to throw the football all the time. He always put one finger on the pointed end of the ball. He taught me to throw it like that. He said it made it go farther.

Willie Thrower: My greatest moment in football was playing against Texas A&M. I went in with four and a half minutes left and threw two touchdown passes. After the game, the Texas A&M coach came to our locker room. He says, "Where's this Willie

Thrower guy?" The players say, "Over there, Number 27." He comes over. "You know what?" he says. "I was proud of my team today—until you stepped into the game. Tell you what," he says. "If they don't give you the game ball, you come to my locker room. I got one for you."

Upon leaving East Lansing, Thrower made his way to Chicago, where he signed on with the Bears as a free agent. On October 18, 1953, he completed three of eight passes for twenty-seven yards in a 35–28 loss to the San Francisco 49ers, becoming the first African American to play quarterback in the NFL. "I was like the Jackie Robinson of football," he told a hometown newspaper. "A black quarterback was unheard of before I hit the pros."

Jim Dooley, former NFL wide receiver: There were only twelve teams in the league, and most kept only two quarterbacks. George Halas had three. He thought enough of Willie to keep him around. The coaches worked very diligently with him. They tried to keep him in the pocket. Willie would leap in the air to throw the ball. Halas would say, "Keep those feet solid on the ground." But Willie had potential. He made the team, even though we had George Blanda and Tommy O'Connell.

Willie Thrower: I got in the San Francisco 49er game as a quarterback after George Halas got dissatisfied with George Blanda. I completed three out of eight passes and took them from our forty-yard line all the way down to about the fifteen. All of a sudden, Halas sends Blanda back in. The fans really jumped on him: "Leave Willie in! Leave Willie in!" But that was it; the end of the game for me.

Jim Dooley: If I recall correctly, Blanda was slightly injured in the second half. He had to come out. The score was close, back and forth, and we had to move the ball. Willie came in full of life. "C'mon, let's do it," he said, and things picked up. Blanda must have been ready to return. That's the only reason I can see to pull Willie late in the drive.

George Blanda: I don't remember getting hurt. I think they decided to put Willie in to see what he could do. Back then, quarterbacks weren't as schooled as they are today. Most of us had been left halfbacks. We learned how to play as we went along. Willie did well. The only reason I can see why he didn't finish the drive is maybe he didn't know the offense that well. We were getting near the goal line, and the coaching staff didn't want to risk anything.

Thrower remained on the bench for all but a handful of minutes in his second game. The Bears released him before the start of the next season. He played four more years in Canada before a separated shoulder ended his career at age twenty-seven. He died of a heart attack at age 71 on February 20, 2002.

Melvin Thrower: He was known here in New Kensington, but he wasn't known downstate in Pittsburgh, in Detroit, in Chicago. Everybody knows Jackie Robinson. My father, they don't know, because he only played in two games. He always used to tell us he was the Jackie Robinson of football, but Jackie Robinson had a career and my dad only played in those two games. When he passed on, that's when people started to realize he was the first black quarterback.

Willie Thrower Jr.: He never bragged on it, so a lot of people didn't believe him. It was only after he passed away that they started hearing the stories on TV. Until then, people didn't believe him, not even in his own hometown. That's the saddest thing about it.

Melvin Thrower: Even some of his friends didn't believe him. My parents owned this bar called The Touchdown Lounge. My dad had a big picture of himself on the wall. On the bottom, it said: THE FIRST BLACK QUARTERBACK IN THE NFL, 1953. People told him to take it down. "You're lying," they said. "You're lying. That ain't you. Take it down."

Weeks after Thrower's historic milestone, another Big Ten alum became the second African-American to complete a pass in the NFL. Indiana's single-wing tailback, George Taliaferro, had also earned the distinction of becoming the first black player selected in the NFL draft, when George Halas' Bears called his name in the thirteenth round in 1949. Taliaferro never did wear a Chicago jersey, though.

George Taliaferro: My father was five-foot-seven-inches tall, 157 pounds. He was the man in our home. He never told me to do anything. He always asked. And I always did what my father asked—except this one time. He asked me to turn over the soil in the empty lot next to our house so he could plant his garden. He wanted me to have it done by the time he got home from work. He worked in the steel mills in Gary, Indiana. I said, "Sure." But I went out and started swimming and forgot all about it. My father got home fifteen minutes after I did. He said to me, "A man is no more, no less than his word."

At one o'clock in the morning, my mother was out there with a lantern while I dug. She said, "Son, you need to eat and you need to go to bed. You can finish this tomorrow." I said, "Mom, he'll never have the opportunity to say that to me again."

When I was drafted by the Bears, my father was dead. I said to my mother, "All I have to do is tear up this contract I signed with the Los Angeles Dons and give them back their $4,000 signing bonus, and I can sign with the Bears."

Do you know what she said?

"What did your father tell you?"

I never said a word to the Bears until 1955, when I finished my career with the Philadelphia Eagles and George Halas called to ask me to play for Chicago. I told him, "Thank you, Mr. Halas, but no thank you. I am no longer the football player that I set the standard for me to be. I am going on with the rest of my life."

And that was it.

The three-time Pro Bowler spent most of his time at running back, finishing with 1,794 rushing yards and ten touchdowns in six NFL seasons. In 1953, however, he started two games at quarterback for the Baltimore Colts, taking the snap from center in a shotgun formation.

George Taliaferro: The team's three quarterbacks had gotten hurt the previous Sunday. On Tuesday, I was walking to the practice field, talking to Gino Marchetti, when head coach Keith Molesworth put his hand on my shoulder and said, "George, have you ever played quarterback?" I said, "Ain't nothing but another position, coach."

There was no free agency. The Colts had to go with what they had, and they had me. I started with four days of practice and damn near beat the Rams. I threw an interception that was returned for a touchdown. That was the difference between winning and losing.

Taliaferro was hurt in the Los Angeles game and attempted just two more passes in his career. The following season, the Colts fired Keith Molesworth and replaced him with Weeb Ewbank. In Ewbank's second year, he drafted George Shaw, an All-America quarterback out of Oregon. Said Taliaferro, "Coach Ewbank would rather tickle King Kong's ass with a feather than give a black player an opportunity to play quarterback."

While Thrower and Taliaferro were smashing barriers inside the NFL, Charlie "Choo Choo" Brackins was luring league scouts to a small college town in Texas, where he piloted the Prairie View A&M Panthers to a 33–4 record in his four years as a starter. More than perceptions, Brackins changed the way the game was played.

Charles Garcia, teammate of Brackins at Prairie View A&M: I once overheard him talking to a scout outside my room. "You want to play at Green Bay?" the scout asks. Choo says, "I just want to play."

Bill Nunn: Choo Choo Brackins had size, the arm, the ability to make it as a pro. Whether or not he could have is open to debate. But, based on the guys I've seen over the years, I'm certain that, given the opportunity, he would have had a very good chance of making it.

Charles Garcia: He was as big as James Harris, but built a little better. He used to alter plays, take things we did in practice and change them during the game. If he saw something on the field, he would switch the play right there. He was thirty years ahead of his time.

My freshman year, we went to Miami to play Florida A&M in the Orange Bowl Classic. Late in the fourth quarter, we were driving down the field. We didn't have any timeouts. Choo took the ball from under center and threw it to the ground. I'd never seen anybody do that before. He got a fifteen-yard penalty for unsportsmanlike conduct.

The Packers took Brackins with the 185th pick in the 1955 draft.

Charles Garcia: Choo went to Green Bay when quarterback Tobin Rote was on the downside. He played in a preseason game, and he went three for five before they pulled him. He wasn't the starter, but the fans would chant his name.

Charles Ross: He's inserted into a couple of games in October. He may throw a pass or two. This is really an interesting case, because the Packers have a very, very bad team and they're really hurting at quarterback. In fact, one sportswriter writes that the Packers' quarterback is one of the most inconsistent in football, and yet they never really give Brackins an opportunity. He's given his unconditional release before the season is out.

In the closing minutes of the season's fifth game in 1955, with Green Bay down 41–10, coach Lisle Blackbourn sent Brackins onto the field to play. Choo Choo threw only two passes, both of them resulting in incompletions. Weeks later, the

Packers cut him, citing violations that included breaking curfew before a game in Chicago. He never played another down in the NFL, and more than a decade would pass before another African-American quarterback was given a chance to play in a pro football game.

Charles Garcia: Choo was electrifying. When he walked into a room, everybody just gravitated to him. But Choo was his own worst enemy. Even in college, he'd go out after curfew. I don't understand why, but he just had to go out.

What I heard was the night before the game against Chicago, he went out and came back the next morning. He's in the elevator with three men connected to the team, and Choo says, "Good morning! How you doin'? Beautiful day for a football game, isn't it?" He did the kickoffs that day. After the game, they cut him loose.

They didn't do their Golden Boys that way. When they caught them gambling, they just suspended them for a year. But Choo was an upbeat guy. In all his days, he never said one bad thing about the Packers.

Less than a decade after Willie Thrower blazed a trail in the Big Ten, Sandy Stephens enrolled at the University of Minnesota, leading the Gophers, who had been a 1–8 team, to two consecutive Rose Bowl appearances in 1961 and 1962. "I was going to be more than a Big Ten quarterback who was black," said Stephens. "I was going to be a Big Ten quarterback who took his team to the Rose Bowl." Wilburn Hollis and Jimmy Raye also led teams to the Big Ten title. But Stephens' 8–1 record in 1960 earned him a national championship.

Wilburn Hollis: Sandy Stephens was very smart and a very hard worker. He insisted on playing quarterback. He refused to go to another position.

Judge Dickson, Gopher fullback: He went to Ohio State and met with Woody Hayes. He was told he would never play quarterback. In Minnesota with coach Murray Warmath, he felt he'd be evaluated by his character, not his color. Warmath used to say the only players he discriminated against were those who could not play football.

Tony Dungy: You have to give Murray Warmath credit. He had this pipeline of his peers. They'd say, "Hey, this guy can't play in the SEC. You ought to take him." He took Carl Eller, Bobby Bell, and Charlie Sanders from North Carolina. And he played Sandy Stephens at quarterback.

Murray Warmath: We didn't just recruit a guy because he was white. You can get a horse's ass no matter which color. We wanted to know what kind of guy he was. Sandy Stephens was strong, determined, smart, and he loved to play. He was the first man to practice, last one off the field. He had so damn much of everything you wanted in a player. He was a great, big, strong son of a bucket who would hurt people if they tried to tackle him.

Judge Dickson: He threw it hard. If you were a receiver and you didn't have strong fingers, you'd have trouble catching the ball.

Murray Warmath: We depended on him a hell of a lot. As a quarterback type, running type, there was nobody better. He had it all, and he was determined to make it.

Judge Dickson: When we were the last-place team in the Big Ten, the local paper ran a big headline, "Minnesota for Minnesota Boys," with pictures of the football players from out of state. Sandy's photo was there. My photo was there. There was definitely a racial component to it. There were those in Minnesota who felt the football team should have blonde hair and blue eyes. They burned Warmath in effigy right outside my window. Killed his dog. Threw garbage on his front lawn. Then we started winning. After the 1962 Rose Bowl against UCLA, both coaches were quoted in the newspaper saying Sandy called the best football game they'd ever seen.

When Sandy made the All-America squad, they wanted him to come to Hershey, Pennsylvania. Sandy told them, "I want to go to the YMCA and swim." When he was in high school, he'd gone to Hershey for the Big 33 All-Star Game, but the local Y wouldn't let him swim because he was black. When he came back to Minnesota, I asked him about the trip. "Dickson," he said, "I'll tell you, I went swimming in that damn pool."

Jimmy Raye followed his hero to the Big Ten in 1965, guiding Michigan State to two Big Ten championships. In 1966, he quarterbacked the second-ranked Spartans against top-ranked Notre Dame in one of the greatest college games of all time. Among those who watched that historic showdown was Tyrone Willingham, who later said, "It was a significant moment in my life, although I didn't know it at the time." Willingham himself would go on to play quarterback for Michigan State and to coach Notre Dame.

Jimmy Raye: I had a little less trepidation than Sandy did at Minnesota, because of Willie Thrower, who had preceded me by some fifteen years. When I went to Michigan State, Duffy Daugherty told my mom I could play quarterback until I decided to switch. Little did I know they were going to make me switch. They told me they were recruiting one other quarterback. When I got there, there were nine and I was number nine. The idea was to bury me so low that, if I wanted to play, I'd say, "Okay, I'll play defensive back." I was the guy picked to scrimmage against the varsity squad so I could get beat up. But I did pretty good. They couldn't deny my ability. The next spring, the list goes up and I'm back down at number eleven. Behind the guys I beat out in freshman ball.

Raye persevered. By the end of the first year, he was the most valuable player on the freshman team. As a sophomore, he waited two weeks for his first snap. At the end of the final scrimmage, he got the chance to run the offense for twenty plays, completing a handful of passes and breaking free on a long run.

Jimmy Raye: I got the snaps, did well, and got to play with the green shirts. If you were in a white shirt, it meant you weren't very good. As Duffy Daugherty got more excited about my ability to run and throw, I got more reps. I'd quarterback the number-one offense down the field, then I'd take my green shirt off and quarterback the scrub team against the number-one defense—Bubba Smith, George Webster, all those guys. I went through all that because I wanted to play. I was determined to play.

He played his way right into history against Notre Dame in what will forever be known as the Game of the Century—a matchup with implications that reached far beyond the record books.

Jimmy Raye: Notre Dame had many great players, but Alan Page was the only black starter. Michigan State started eight blacks on defense. The offensive backfield was all black, except for the fullback. Gene Washington was the wide receiver.

When I was Michigan State's starting quarterback, Duffy Daugherty used to use the word "indelible." He said, "Your name will be written in indelible ink. It will stand the test of time." Little did I know that forty years later, people would still be talking about that 10–10 tie—a game we didn't win.

Despite the early slights from Daugherty, Raye forged a lifelong friendship with his college coach. "The things he did to me, he had to do because of the times and the pressure on him," Raye said. "He used to show me some of the mail he got."

Within five years, quarterback Willie Wood and tailback Sam "Bam" Cunningham of USC lay a convincing beating on Bear Bryant's Alabama Crimson Tide, paving the way for integrated rosters throughout the South. Inside the draft rooms of the NFL, however, black quarterbacks were still viewed as budding receivers and defensive backs. Among those called upon to make the switch in the pro ranks were Michigan State's Sherman Lewis, Illinois' Mel Meyers, and Iowa's Wilburn Hollis, who led the Hawkeyes to a share of the Big Ten title in 1960.

For Sandy Stephens, that option was a clear slap in the face. The Cleveland Browns selected him in the second round in 1961. The AFL's New York Titans picked him in round one. He lit out for Canada, instead, to play for the Montreal Alouettes. He played briefly with the Toronto Argonauts, too. In 1964, he returned to the United States for a tryout with the Minnesota Vikings. On the night before his session, his hopes were dashed in a car accident.

Judge Dickson: Sandy was in a convertible with Ted Dean, who played for the Eagles and Vikings, on Cedar Avenue in Minneapolis, late at night. He ran into a tree at a very high speed. They brought Sandy into the hospital in a paper bag. He had internal injuries, broken bones, everything. There was a question about whether he'd live, never mind walk.

He worked hard at the rehabilitation. His dream was to be a quarterback in the NFL. And Hank Stram, who had been an assistant coach at Purdue, gave Sandy a look-see with the Chiefs. I went out to see him at the last preseason game. He started and played well. But the Chiefs had to cut one more player and Sandy was the one. It punched a hole in him. How do you get up off the ground again and again? How long can you keep fighting?

In 1997, nearly three decades after he played his last football game, Stephens was inducted into the Rose Bowl Hall of Fame. Three years later, he died of a heart attack. In a letter read at his memorial service, the Reverend Jesse Jackson said, "[Sandy] made us feel so proud, with his poise and dignity, as well as his athletic ability. I am convinced his dreams of having an even playing field for his skills to be demonstrated were broken, but his non-negotiable dignity and private pride were never broken."

Marlin Briscoe, 1968.

CHAPTER FOUR

1968

Political upheaval. Assassinations. Social unrest. The year 1968 was a pivotal one in the United States. There was a minor upheaval in professional football as well: Three African-American quarterbacks—Eldridge Dickey, Marlin Briscoe, and Jimmy Raye— entered an arena poised for change, albeit at different positions. Dickey, who—like Joe Gilliam—had starred at Tennessee State, was selected as an "athlete" by the AFL's Oakland Raiders with the twenty-fifth overall pick, marking the first time an African-American QB was chosen in the first round. And Marlin Briscoe, from the University of Omaha, and Jimmy Raye, the outstanding Michigan State quarterback, were drafted as defensive backs—Briscoe in the fourteenth round by the AFL's Denver Broncos and Raye in the sixteenth round by the NFL's Rams. Raye was traded to the Philadelphia Eagles, where, a year later, he played in two games before retiring from football. (Decades later, he would break a different barrier, becoming the first African-American offensive coordinator, calling plays for the Chiefs, Buccaneers, Rams, Patriots, Raiders, and Redskins.)

Dickey, who led Tennessee State to bowl berths in 1965 and 1966, boasted a strong arm and the ability to make plays on the move. He believed he was going to be the first African-American quarterback to play and perhaps even start on a regular basis.

Gene Upshaw: There was no other organization [than the Raiders] that was willing to take that chance. I mean, just think about it. Who was going to draft this guy from Tennessee State in the first round? It was unheard-of.

Marlin Briscoe: That was Al Davis' deal. Al always wanted to be the first in anything related to football history. He always wanted to create a stir. So I think he was looking at the talent Dickey had—he didn't care about the color of his skin.

David Meggyesy, former Cardinals linebacker, author, *Out of Their League*: The American Football League came on the scene, and they needed players. They didn't care who. Color was not an issue.

John Rauch, former Raiders coach: As the owner and managing general partner, Al Davis was very instrumental in the final decision. But everybody—our general manager and all of our scouts—was involved in deciding who we were going to draft. Eldridge Dickey had great athletic skills. If we needed a quarterback, he could play quarterback. If we needed a running back, he could play running back. If we needed a wide receiver, he could play wide receiver—any skilled position on offense. And that's mainly why Dickey was drafted by the Raiders.

Even though Dickey practiced with the quarterbacks during training camp, the Raiders had him slotted as a wide receiver and paid him more to accept the switch. At camp, he excelled as a QB, and, according to some, outplayed Alabama's Ken Stabler, who was the team's second-round pick that same year.

Gene Upshaw: I'd never seen a guy who could do what Dickey did with both hands and both feet. It was just amazing. He didn't go to Alabama. He hadn't won any national championships. But when he went out on the field and started throwing the ball, you could see he had more ability than Stabler. He shows up, and he's got these white shoes. And he's doing his shit, making it look easy. Blocking for him was hard because he was always moving around. All of a sudden, he'd be out of that pocket. Gone! Nowadays, with Michael Vick, Donovan McNabb, Steve McNair, it's okay to leave the pocket, but not then. We were used to Daryle Lamonica, who was a statue—just stood back there. There was no way in the world to know where Dickey was going to be. What we did know was that he was breaking down barriers, and we worked our asses off to make sure he succeeded. That's one thing I got to say about Al Davis: He would not tolerate racism. In fact, Stabler believed that Davis was giving Dickey the better chance to succeed. That's why Stabler went off to some team in Spokane. He left the team for a year.

Art Shell, former Raiders tackle: Snake had a problem with his knee, plus some issues at home, as I recall. All of a sudden, he's not there. I think he played in a semipro league. Dickey was one of the most talented players I've ever seen. The guy could throw with his left hand just as good as he could with his right. I've never seen nothing like it. He could have done anything he wanted to do. But looking back on it, I think he was spoiled coming out of Tennessee State. He didn't feel he needed to put forth the effort to become a quarterback in the NFL. He had his white buck shoes and his black Eldorado, but I don't think he was ready to study. I don't think he was taught how to study.

Joe Gilliam Sr.: Dickey threw a lot of interceptions, but he made up for it with his legs. Many times, he would drop back with no intention of passing. He was going to run it from the very beginning. He was good at that.

John Rauch: We had Daryle Lamonica, George Blanda, and Cotton Davidson at quarterback. Ken Stabler had a tough time competing against them. They all had been in pro football for years. Kenny didn't make the team his first or second year with the Raiders. The first year, he had a knee operation, and he had marital problems that had him confused, and he had to drop out. He wasn't cut. He just dropped out. The second year, he was the fourth-string quarterback, so we sent him up to Spokane, Washington, and played in the Continental Football League. You got all of these quarterbacks, and where are you going to put Eldridge Dickey? Well, if he can't beat out any one of them, you're going to play him where he has a chance to make the team. So we looked at him as a halfback. Wide receiver, too.

Gene Upshaw: It started going bad because the coaches wanted Dickey in the pocket. Same shit we hear now. They wanted to make him a prototype quarterback. Dickey would stay in there for a while, then he'd say, "Shit, I'm gone." They tried to make him a wide receiver, but he was never really the same. He wasn't a receiver. He was too goddamn big, number one. And number two, he had too much ability. He could throw to the other end of the field.

Marlin Briscoe: Each position has a different mind-set. As the quarterback, you're a leader. When you're a wide receiver, you're isolated out there. You have to be graceful and smooth and all that stuff. The change had to be hard for him.

Gene Upshaw: It would be like telling you all of a sudden, "No, you ain't a writer, you're a construction worker." It had to have an effect. He never really got a chance to be what he thought he should be. And it was only because of where we were in time.

Dickey played in eleven games his rookie year, catching one ball for thirty-four yards. Injuries kept him out of the next two seasons. In 1971, he caught four passes for seventy-eight yards and a touchdown. It was his final year in the league.

Gene Upshaw: Eldridge had some abilities, but looking back, I'm not so sure he—or the Raiders coaching staff—knew what it took to succeed. They just didn't give it enough time. I mean, the year before Dickey came to the Raiders, Lamonica went 13–1 as a quarterback, and we went to the Super Bowl. Whatever Eldridge did was going to be compared to that. He had to be All-World right away. Al was fighting for him, but the coaches were saying, "Well, he's not doing this." They didn't understand. They had never coached a black quarterback.

"Should we kick him in the ass? Should we make him do what every-one else is doing? Should we let him be a prima donna?" They didn't know what to do. They were afraid. There was a learning curve on both sides.

It wasn't Dickey but the obscure Briscoe who would impress AFL observers in '68. Standing just five-foot-eleven and 185 pounds, Marlin Briscoe was nick-named The Magician for his ability to elude defenders and make plays on the move. He finished his senior year at the University of Omaha with 2,283 yards passing and was named an NAIA All-America. Still, when the Broncos signed Briscoe, it was as a defensive back. On the advice of his college coach, Briscoe insisted that his contract call for at least a look-see at quarterback. He arrived at camp to discover he was number eight out of eight on the QB depth chart.

Marlin Briscoe: When I got drafted in the fourteenth round by Denver, they wanted me to play cornerback. My college coach Al Caniglia had played with the Green Bay Packers, and he told me, "Listen, Denver is one of the only teams in the NFL that practices in the city, where the media and the fans can watch. See if you can insert a little trial—two or three days—at quarterback in your contract." I thought it was a great idea. When Stan Jones came to negotiate the contract, I said, "You know, I'll sign the contract if Denver gives me a three-day trial. All I want to do is test my skills out for three days." Well, Stan liked me. He told Broncos coach Lou Saban he thought I could play quarterback, but Saban wouldn't have it. Neither would Fred Gehrke [the director of player personnel]. He said, "No way!" They thought I was nuts. Well, the contract was worth only $15,000 a year. So I said, "I can get a teaching job." I wanted to play football, but I was adamant about that three-day trial. Finally, they acquiesced.

During those three days, I had a heck of a camp. Coach Caniglia had prepared me for the challenge. He gave me information, the confidence to go in there and perform well. We had eight quarterbacks, and I was always the last one up. If they each got ten throws, I'd get only five. But I'd known it wasn't going to be fair. So when I was called upon to make my five throws, I had to make the best of it. After three days, the *Denver Post* wrote a big article on me. Talked about my college career. So I got what I wanted.

After starter Steve Tensi broke his collarbone, two of the eight quarterbacks in that trial were given his job. They failed. So Briscoe got his shot. Facing the Boston Patriots in week three, he entered the game with Denver down 20–7 and nearly pulled out a victory, rushing for a touchdown as the Broncos fell 20–17.

Marlin Briscoe: The offense hadn't scored a touchdown since Tensi went down. The fans and the media started saying, "Well, why don't you let Briscoe play?" The fans and the media pressured Saban. That's how it all started.

I got in for the last ten minutes against Boston. We were down maybe two touchdowns. I only had, like, six or seven plays, and I guess they figured, with six or seven plays, there's not much I could do. I completed my first pass. I knew I had to do that. I sliced it to Eric Crabtree—I will never forget that—and the crowd went wild. We go down the field, and I scramble into the end zone. I almost pulled the game out. So there was a buzz around the city. The next week, droves of fans showed up.

Head coach Lou Saban begrudgingly named Briscoe the starter for game four against Cincinnati, making him the first black quarterback to start a professional game. He played in eleven games that season—including seven starts—and set a Broncos' rookie record of 14 TDs, while amassing 1,589 yards passing and 308 yards rushing. He finished second to Cincinnati running back Paul Robinson for AFL Rookie of the Year.

Marlin Briscoe: I look in my locker and see this Number 15 jersey. I was Number 20, I think. Back in those days, when they cut somebody, they just took his stuff out of the locker. You'd go to your locker, and if your jersey and your stuff weren't there, that meant you were cut. I knew the quarterback situation was dire and that they'd probably make a trade for somebody. So when I saw that Number 15 jersey in my locker, I thought I'd been cut. I turn around, and here comes Lou Saban. He says, "Briscoe, you see that Number 15? Well, it's yours. You're a quarterback now." My heart jumped. I couldn't believe it. I mean, it was just unbelievable. I had maybe five days to prepare for the game. I had done all this physical stuff in the three-day trial, but we didn't have playbooks. I had limited information. So I just pretended I was back in college. I knew I was going to have to be able to run and throw until I got more information.

Al Denson, former Broncos receiver: Marlin was electrifying. They couldn't touch him because he was so good in the backfield—better than Fran Tarkenton. Marlin was short, and it was hard for him to throw over the linemen, but he was real accurate. In those days, we played straight man-to-man, bump-and-run, and deep zone coverage. The defenders could go over your head and beat you half to death. If you caught fifty passes, you were great. I think Marlin completed, like, seventy percent of his passes that day and gained eighty yards scrambling. He really put us on the map.

Paul Warfield, former Dolphins receiver: He was an athletic player—and he needed that athleticism because Denver's line was not very good. In the face of all that pressure, he held his composure. He wasn't fazed by the linebackers and defensive linemen coming free. He had great escape skills. He made plays from the pocket, but he made plays on the run, too.

Floyd Little, former Broncos running back: He was incredible. Running with the ball, he was like Barry Sanders. Today, you look at Michael Vick, and you see Marlin Briscoe, forty years removed. Marlin wasn't as quick as Vick, but he had a better arm.

Marlin Briscoe: I almost beat the Raiders in game thirteen. I threw three touchdown passes in the first half, and we had them on the ropes. On the last play of the half, I was going for broke, trying to get another one, when Ben Davidson knocked me silly. I came out for the second half but wasn't as effective. They came back. I threw six touchdown passes in two games against the Chargers. With Lance Alworth and John Hadl, they had a really exciting offense. I almost beat them. Then I beat the Dolphins. I always remind Bob Griese of that: I beat him head-to-head. That game was huge. Everybody came out to see the duel of the scramblers, and I beat him on a ten-yard quarterback sneak. I checked off the play, and we won in the last few minutes by running it in. The players gave me a lot of respect for that. Back in '68, most of the linemen were white. A lot of them came from Southern schools. Not only had they never played with a black quarterback, they'd never played with black players. So it was a huge adjustment. But they gave me a lot of respect for checking off on that play.

Floyd Little: We were at home against the Bills. We had the lead and the ball late in the game. I was running right, trying to stay in bounds, and I tripped over the turf. I don't know how it happened, but the ball slipped out of my arm.

Marlin Briscoe: We had come from behind and were running out the clock. I sent Floyd on a sweep, and he fumbled. The Bills get the ball back and score a touchdown to go ahead.

Floyd Little: On the sideline, Saban said, "I want you outta here. You're fired." I was on the return team, and he wouldn't let me return the kickoff. He told me I was done. "I-70 runs east and west, and I-25 runs north and south," he said. "You can get on any one of them. You're through with the Broncos. Finished." I was furious. I went walking to the locker room and got right near the end zone, when I decided I wasn't going to go out like that. I spun around and ran into the huddle. Fran Lynch, my roommate, was in the game. I said, "Fran, I need you to do me a favor: Get off the field!"

Marlin Briscoe: We got the ball for one more try, and I have this play in mind. I'm going to throw to Floyd out of the backfield because I figure they'll double up on my receiver. I look to the sideline, and here comes

Fran Lynch—Fran couldn't run a seven-flat forty—so that play's going to be nullified. Well, all of a sudden, Floyd runs onto the field, and Fran goes off. I'm running out of time, so I call the play. They flushed me out of the pocket. I rolled left and threw the ball sixty-six yards in the air with Floyd streaking down the field—perfect. I threw it from one side of the field to the other. Caught him in stride.

Floyd Little: He's rolling to his left, and I'm streaking down the sideline, and I can see everybody going toward Marlin. Marlin was in a pile of people, and all of a sudden, I see this rocket come out of the pile. The pass went over sixty yards. The Bills were in a prevent defense. The next thing I know, there's three or four guys on me: George Saimes, Booker Edgerson, John Pitts, who's about six-three, six-four. I went up and caught the ball. They tried to strip it from me. I was beaten up, just torn up. The referee threw a flag for unnecessary roughness and marched the ball down to the ten-yard line with about five seconds to go. Bobby Howfield comes in for the field goal. I'm in agony on the sideline, waiting. He kicks it through, and everybody is hollering and cheering. I'm walking toward the locker room, and Coach calls me over. I tell him to take a hike, in so many words. He says, "I'm gonna give you one more week." I stayed for nine more years. Marlin saved my job.

Marlin Briscoe: After my rookie year, I decided to go home to Omaha and get my degree. I needed six credit hours to graduate. My cousin Bob Rose had moved to Denver with me. He calls me up and tells me the Broncos have signed Pete Liske from Canada, and they're having quarterback meetings. I said, "What do you mean they're having quarterback meetings? They never told me about quarterback meetings." Here I am, the starting quarterback at year's end, and they don't even invite me. So I took a clandestine flight to Denver. I stood outside the coach's office, and out walks Steve Tensi, Lou Saban, quarterback coach Hunter Anderson, Pete Liske, and a couple quarterbacks. They couldn't even look at me. If I didn't think it was wrong for a man to cry, I'd have cried. I was that hurt. I just turned and walked out. I knew I wasn't in their plans. It was like I'd never played that first year.

Floyd Little: We were football players. As long as we won, we didn't care about the color of the quarterback. Marlin was the best we had. We all rallied around him—everybody on the team. We were competitive. Shit, we were moving the ball, getting it in the end zone. We had the coaches off our asses. The greatest thing in the world was giving Marlin the opportunity to be quarterback. We all thought he'd be our quarterback the next season. But the coach had different plans. He had given up so much for Steve Tensi—two number-one draft choices. You can't give up two first-round draft choices and not play the guy. We went through five or six quarterbacks that year. Tensi, Jim LeClair, John McCormick. If Lou had stayed with Marlin, our chances would have been better. But I don't think the league was ready for a black quarterback.

Lou Saban: Marlin was an exceptional athlete, but he didn't have great size. He was always throwing out of a well. I figured his best position was receiver, but we were searching for a quarterback. In the four and a half years I was with the Broncos, we never found a guy who could take over the position. We brought in quarterbacks by the dozens. It didn't make much difference what their backgrounds were, I was going to play whoever could win—because if you don't win, it's over.

Floyd Little: Marlin didn't have a problem with management, he had a problem with Saban. He bumped heads with a goat. Coach Saban ruled with an iron hand. He would grab guys by the face mask. He was always screaming, "My grandmother's better than you." One time, he fired the whole kickoff team. We were at Rice Stadium, playing Houston, and the game was nip and tuck. We kicked a field goal, kicked the ball back to them, and they ran it back just before the half. The score was 6–3, and Saban was furious. During halftime, he kicked over a table that had oranges, Gatorade, and water on it. "Nothing for you guys at halftime," he said. Everyone on the kickoff team had to raise their hand. He counted them off and said, "Okay, get your shit. You're done." The kicker asked him who was gonna kick off after halftime. "I will," he said. "You're fired. You're all fired." I liked Saban. He and I had the same personality. But he was a bastard, a slave master. He made all of the decisions.

Marlin Briscoe: I was labeled a malcontent. It wasn't like I went to the press, and it wasn't like I ranted and raved. I quietly said, "Hey, I deserve to play this position. If I had failed, I'd see your side of it. But you're not even giving me the opportunity after I proved I can play the position and play it well." That's the way I was raised. My mother said, "If you feel you're right, stand up for yourself."

Roy S. Johnson: Imagine if a rookie quarterback comes in today, throws fourteen touchdown passes, piles up 1,600 yards. You're looking at someone who's entrenched in that position for a decade, the future of the franchise.

Floyd Little: Was Marlin selfish? I don't know. He had such a great season, they should have given him some kind of bonus. It wouldn't have been all that much. My bonus at the end of the year was five hundred bucks. But Marlin got to be pretty adamant about wanting more money. He was not in a negotiating mood. He wasn't willing to compromise. It was an ultimatum. I don't do ultimatums. Somebody gives me an ultimatum, it's an automatic no. I don't care what it is. That's been my deal for fifty years. If you say, "You'll do this or that's it," then that's it for me. And like I said, Lou Saban and I have the same personality. Here was a man who once challenged the whole team to a fight in the locker room. We were in Salt Lake City playing the Patriots. At halftime, Lou rolled up his sleeves, clenched his fists, and started pointing fingers at everyone. He said he would kick everybody's ass, that we were a bunch of gutless thieves. This is a guy you don't box in.

Marlin Briscoe: I asked Saban to let me go. He said, "Okay, but you have to wait four days." I'm trying to figure out why. After those four days, no team would touch me. I went to Canada, the BC Lions, and I didn't like Canadian football. I felt I belonged in the NFL. So I started calling around to the teams I had success against in '68. I'd beaten Buffalo once and almost beat Oakland, and Raiders coach John Rauch was now in Buffalo.

John Rauch: We were at training camp at the University of Niagara, as I remember it, discussing personnel. At some point I said, "We've got to find some wide receivers." Just then, one of our scouts came into the office and said, "I have a call from Vancouver. Marlin Briscoe is on the phone." And I thought, This is interesting—we were just discussing this situation, and here comes a phone call from Marlin Briscoe, asking for an opportunity to get back to the United States. I knew about him, had read the reports and seen films of him. He could run with the football and had great speed.

Marlin Briscoe: He picked up the phone. Talked to me directly.

John Rauch: I explain our situation: I'm loaded at quarterback, but I'm interested in a wide receiver. He says, "I'll be there in a day or two." And he was. He paid his own way to New York and came to Niagara in a little more than twenty-four hours. Well, it was obvious the guy was talented. He had no problem picking up our system, no problem running pass routes. Pretty impressive record as a wide receiver too, enough so that the Miami Dolphins gave up a number one draft choice for him after I left the Bills.

Marlin Briscoe: He said he didn't need a quarterback, only a receiver. But Jack Kemp was hurt, Tom Flores was hurt, and Shack Harris was hurt. So he did need somebody to throw in camp. Once again, I negotiated my own contract. I said, "Okay, I'll play wide receiver, but you can't cut me until the very last cut." I'm not going to come in for a couple of days, then get cut at a position I'd never played.

By day, he played quarterback. At night, he worked on his receiving skills.

Marlin Briscoe: I knew I was good enough to make the transition, but how was I going to devote half the day to throwing and still learn what I had to learn? I had to find somebody to ape. So I got clips of Paul Warfield and Lance Alworth and studied those at night. I had ten days to make the team. So I stayed up watching film, studying their moves. I thought I could mirror them. I had been working with receivers all my life. I knew how the position was supposed to be played. And handling the ball so much, I had developed good hands and a feel for the ball. What I had to learn was how to run patterns. I was always quick on my feet, but I never had to use breakaway speed, straightaway speed. So that was a liability. But I felt I belonged in the NFL. So I was driven to make that transition. All I needed was time. Bill Miller, the receivers coach, worked hard with me during that stretch. And I have to give him a lot of credit, because I could tell by his body language and his dialogue that he really wanted me to make it. He worked extra hard with me after practice. He was really patient.

Against the L.A. Rams in the last exhibition game of the preseason, they put me in. Jack Kemp was the quarterback. He knew my plight. He and I were roommates on the road. When I walked into the huddle, we had about ten minutes left. He said, "Well, I'll throw you the ball." He kept throwing me the ball, and I kept catching it. At the end of the day, I was the team's leading receiver. They couldn't cut me.

Briscoe blossomed into a quality receiver with the Bills, earning a trip to the 1971 Pro Bowl following a campaign in which he caught fifty-seven passes for

1,036 yards and eight TDs. His old nemesis Lou Saban was named head coach for the 1972 season and traded him to the Dolphins soon thereafter. Briscoe was a member of the 17–0 Dolphins squad that remains the only undefeated team in NFL history. The itch to quarterback never left him, and he was able to scratch it sporadically in Miami.

Marlin Briscoe: After practice, Paul Warfield had me throw to him. Don Shula put pass plays in the playbook for me, and when Griese went down, Shula had enough respect to make me the emergency quarterback. The fact that he knew I could fill the void was gratifying but frustrating. If I was good enough to be an emergency quarterback, why weren't other teams willing to give me a chance?

Paul Warfield: Marlin was not only a good pass receiver, but he also had the ability to advance the ball considerably after the catch. You'd throw him a short pass, and the defense would come up to the line immediately. The coaching staff saw that we could use this to put maximum pressure on the defense. Today, you see quarterbacks flip a quick pass to a receiver to give him a chance to show his running ability. The special play the coaching staff devised for Marlin was similar. I was the slot receiver. Marlin lined up one yard off the line. The quarterback would throw him a quick hitch pass—actually, a lateral. I'd run downfield toward one of the two defenders, under control, kind of like a blocker. As soon as they came toward me, I'd release downfield, and Marlin would deliver the football. It put tremendous pressure on the defense, put them in a bind.

*After stints with the Lions, Chargers, and Patriots, Marlin Briscoe retired in
1976. He later battled drug addiction and beat it. Eldridge Dickey wasn't
so lucky.*

Paul Warfield: In my mind, a champion is someone who has the
ability to rise above adverse situations and there have been a number of times in Marlin's life when he was faced with challenges that
appeared to be insurmountable. He's not a quitter. He always finds
a way to bounce back and succeed.

Marlin Briscoe: When Oakland came to visit us in Denver, Eldridge
Dickey came to my apartment. He was introduced by a friend from
the Raiders. A lot of people who had seen him play had heaped a lot
of praise on him. We had a couple players on the Broncos who had
just left Oakland. They were talking about this kid Dickey. We had
several black players from all-black colleges who had played against
Dickey. They called him the Lord's Prayer. He had quite a reputation. He did okay as a receiver, but he wanted to play his natural
position: quarterback. When he came to my house, I could tell that
things didn't sit right with him. He really wanted to be the first black
quarterback, and should have been, to be honest with you. But for
some reason—divine intervention, whatever—he wasn't. You could
see it in his demeanor. That something was denied him. He wasn't
bitter toward me, but I sensed something in his body language.

Gene Upshaw: When I heard he had died, in 2000, I was shocked. He
was too young. Eldridge loved Eldridge. He never messed around. I
thought about the white shoes. I thought about his Cadillac. I thought

about his nickname: the Lord's Prayer. I thought about him out on the field in the Coliseum. He would see something, and all of a sudden, he'd be gone. Out of there.

He never really had a chance, because in those days, they didn't give you a chance. You're in the moment, and you don't have a point of reference because there's no one else in front of you.

Being a pioneer is a bitch.

James Harris, 1976.

CHAPTER FIVE

SHACK

J ames "Shack" Harris was born in 1947, in Monroe, Louisiana, where he experienced suffocating segregation. His mother worked for a white doctor, and while that gave him certain access, it came at a price, leaving Harris particularly aware of the racism all around him. He learned not only how to get by, but how to excel. By the time he got to Grambling, he possessed a well-grounded, unflappable presence. And yet, the pro game required a major adjustment. When Harris stepped into his first pro huddle with the Buffalo Bills, in the summer of 1969, he thought that he was about to talk to more whites at once than at any other time in his life. Not only that, he would be giving them orders.

James Harris: Racism was a way of life in Monroe. My old man was a preacher, and going to church every Sunday, you'd pass all these white churches, hear the preachers say all men are created equal. We lived close to the Little League stadium. I'd lie in my bed and hear them calling the white boys' names on this big speaker. *And at second base.…*We'd go there sometimes and look over the fence—see them walking around in them fine uniforms. We couldn't play. Those daily denials chip away at your manhood. They erode self-confidence. You saw people who challenged segregation go to jail, get beaten, or come up missing. They'd be floating down the river, and you'd ask yourself, How is it that all men are created equal?

I was a good student, making straight A's in school, so I decided I was going to be president of the United States. Then we get to these big words in fourth grade. I'll never forget, the word *assassination* came up. From that day on, my future was in sports. I didn't know about the money. I didn't think about money. It was all about making something out of my life. I used to follow the big boys to the park to play sandlot football. No pads. Toughest guys I ever saw. On TV, wasn't no blacks playing quarterback. So I made sure I was a running back, made sure I was Jim Brown. The quarterback position was appealing—calling the signals, being the leader—but I knew there was no future in it.

Life was simple. You went to school. You worked at home. You went to church. In between, you played sports. One summer, I'm out there working in the cotton fields and I hear my mother talking to some people about college. I didn't know anything about college—in my neighborhood, you finished school and you started working. Either that or you went to jail or the Army. Well, it was 130 degrees in this cotton field, and people were wearing long shirts and these robes. I started thinking, This is what I'll be doing the rest of my life. That's when it hit me: college.

My folks weren't football people. My father liked baseball. My mother swore there would be no more football after my older brother broke his collarbone. I went out for my high school team anyway. I'm competing with the starter as a sophomore, and the coach gives me a ball to take home so I can work on my throwing. My mom wanted to know why I always had that football around. I couldn't tell her.

It gets to the point where the coach can't decide who to start. We flip a coin, and I end up winning. I'm going to start the game that Friday night, and my mother doesn't even know I'm playing.

At Carroll High School in Monroe, Harris led the football team to thirty-nine straight victories and began to think seriously about his dream of becoming a professional athlete. His coach convinced his mother that her youngest son was good enough to earn a scholarship. While establishing himself as a prime college prospect, Harris went to Fayetteville, North Carolina, one summer to visit his older brother, who was in the service and stationed at Fort Bragg. That's where he met two-sport star Jimmy Raye.

James Harris: I was a basketball player deluxe, so we start playing, mixing it up. All of a sudden, people are coming from near and far to see me play basketball against Jimmy Raye.

Jimmy Raye: I remember the first time I met him. I was at home asleep. These kids came and woke me up: "You got to come see this guy. He can really shoot the basketball." I was arguably the best player in the state at the time, so I go down there, and Shack says, "Let two great hands meet," and he shook his own hand. Well, word spread that the game was on at Seabrook Park. We'd have a thousand people show up just to watch.

James Harris: Next thing I know, they're trying to recruit me to play high school basketball in North Carolina. They didn't know I played football.

A year later, on August 28, 1963, Martin Luther King delivered his I Have a Dream speech on the steps of the Lincoln Memorial. Sixteen-year-old James Harris watched the march on TV, and King's words resonated with him.

James Harris: I'm thinking about college, watching games on TV, and I keep hearing about all these guys in the Big Ten who switched positions. A guy from my high school went to Grambling, then made it with the Cleveland Browns—as a defensive back. I figure I've got to switch positions if I'm going to play pro ball. A couple of guys from Monroe thumbed up north for the March on Washington, and I was looking for them on TV. I heard Martin Luther King say that one day it will not be the color of your skin; it will be the content of your character. That's when I decided I wasn't going to switch. I started thinking, Blacks are going to play quarterback.

Harris received letters from all over, but there wasn't much interest in his arm. He visited Michigan State, where Jimmy Raye was a rising star on the freshman football team.

Jimmy Raye: I can remember practicing the days that Shack was there. He was with the coach, who was recruiting him, leaning against the seven-man sled. Someone threw an errant pass in his direction, and he reached up with one hand, caught the ball, and threw it back.

James Harris: I was trying to show off. I played catch so much I could do all kinds of tricks. When the coach who was recruiting me introduced me to Duffy Daugherty, he told Duffy, "He's got a natural throwing arm but great hands." It was obvious what they were going to do.

Jimmy Raye: Shack was adamant about being a quarterback. That's why, when he left, he said, "The next time you see me, I'll be on the cover of *Sports Illustrated*."

James Harris: Grambling coach Eddie Robinson was producing a lot of NFL players. One night, he came to my house to recruit me. He had just been to New York to do a TV show with Howard Cosell, and Cosell asked him point-blank, "You're producing all these players. Why can't you produce a quarterback?" That got to Coach Robinson. He told me if I came to Grambling, I'd be ready for the NFL when I left. He said, "Howard Cosell challenged me, and I think you could be the one."

Jerry Izenberg: Eddie calls me on the phone one day and says, "I need you to do me a favor and go to a bookstore. I need you to get me a copy of Bart Starr's book on quarterbacking." I had it in my house. I said, "I'll send it to you. What's this all about?" He said, "Well, I saw this long, tall boy who runs like a stork, and I think he could be a quarterback. I'm going to recruit that boy for Grambling." He had me come down to write some pieces about this kid he thought could be the first black quarterback in the NFL.

Charles Ross: Eddie Robinson wasn't simply a football coach; he was a surrogate father to his players. He wanted to prepare them for the tough realities they'd find when they left school. It was no coincidence that Tank Younger, the first African-American signed from a black college, had played for Robinson at Grambling. Robinson prepared him very carefully for the reality that he wasn't going to encounter a level playing field when he got to the NFL. He was going to have to clear some hurdles that the average white player wasn't subjected to. Robinson gave Tank the tools he needed to get it done. He did the same thing with James Harris.

Jerry Izenberg: Robinson's preparation was unbelievable. He called me one day after Grambling had played in New York and said, "I want you to do me a favor." I had taken him to Mike Manucci's, this restaurant next to the old Americana. A lot of Giants football players ate there. He said, "I want you to go to Manucci's and a couple of other places—seafood, steak, whatever. I want you to get the menus and send them to me. I'll get Mrs. So-and-so in the dining hall to see what she can make, have her set up plates with forks and knives and everything. I don't want the players to be embarrassed to order food when they walk into a big-city restaurant."

Charlie Joiner, former Grambling teammate: Shack was a master storyteller. We'd be at the student union with a bunch of guys, and he's the focal point because he's doing all the talking. He liked to brag about what he did at Carroll High, how good his team was. That's James to me. Even today, if you go to the Indy combine, it's the same thing. He's always got people around him, and he's telling stories. That's how I picture James Harris: telling stories and laughing.

Harold Jackson, former Rams teammate: When he was around the guys—his peers—he'd always be talking. I'll tell you, everybody from Grambling, they're all the same way: the biggest bullshitters. Tank Younger was always bull-jiving with the players. At Grambling, there must have been a course in bullshitting. They all took it.

Charlie Joiner: Shack put the ball in a position where you could make a good catch. There was very seldom a poorly-thrown ball. One game our sophomore year, Shack says, "Look, Charlie, run this post corner precisely right and I'll put it in your left hip pocket." I'm about twenty-five yards deep, and I turn and come out of the post, and the ball is right there on my left hip. I'm telling you, he was that good—right on my left hip. Honest truth. I will always remember that. It was a touchdown, and it was against Lem Barney—who became one of the better corners in the NFL.

Harold Jackson: I went to Jackson State, so we played against each other in college. One year, the game was at Jackson, and there must have been 40,000 folks in the stands. Shack was out of the pocket, running to the sideline. He was out of bounds, and somebody knocked him right up against the brick wall at Memorial Coliseum. I thought he was really messed up, but he got up. Shack was that tough.

From 1966 through 1968, Harris led Grambling to a 24–5–1 record and three consecutive SWAC championships. But his NFL prospects were limited. Raye was a defensive back in the pros. Dickey and Briscoe would soon be converted to wide receivers. After being drafted in the eighth round by the Buffalo Bills, a disappointed Harris lived in fear during training camp, waiting for the inevitable bad news.

James Harris: They didn't draft me the first day. All these guys I'd played against in the SWAC were getting picked. What chance did I have? I decided I wasn't going to play. Coach called me and said he wanted to talk. We went out to the bleachers, just me and him, sat down, and I told him that being from the segregated South, understanding that no blacks were playing quarterback, I couldn't see any reason to go to Buffalo. He said, "I know you can play quarterback in the NFL. The decision is yours, but if you don't go, if guys like you don't go, it's going to be that much more difficult for the next guy." That touched me.

Jimmie Giles: Coach Robinson always talked about living in America. If you want something, you've gotta understand how to go out and get it. He was not a negative person, always positive.

Willie Davis, former Grambling defensive end: No one was better than Coach Robinson at convincing you that somehow you could do something. I can still see and hear him saying things meant to prepare you for whatever challenge you faced.

James Harris: I made a commitment, threw balls 'til my arm got sore. They always talked about the down-and-out in the NFL, so I went to the park—nobody there but me—to test myself. I was going to throw at this tree blindfolded. I figured if I hit the tree, I'm ready. If I miss the tree, I've got to walk and get the ball. The first time I tried, I missed. The ball was way downfield. I debated about trying it again. I dropped back and threw, heard the ball hit, and something went through me—gave me all the confidence in the world.

John Rauch: When I was with Oakland, I tried to get Roman Gabriel from the Rams, and James Harris reminded me of Roman Gabriel. You have scouts on the road watching college players, meeting them, meeting their coaches and their families, and they bring back these elaborate reports. You spend hours, day and night, going through these reports. And from the reports and the films I saw after I took over as coach of the Bills, James Harris reminded me of Roman Gabriel. The very first time I saw him play, I said, "There's Roman Gabriel." Same physique. Same abilities. So we drafted James Harris.

James Harris: Coach was doing my contract. This guy comes to Grambling and offers me a $1,500 bonus. He wants to watch me throw. He goes off to make a phone call. Comes back and tells me, "I called and told them you're better than we thought." Offers me $500 more. Coach thought about it. Told me to get up to Buffalo and work out because there were other players there. Told them I wasn't supposed to talk contracts. When I got there, they picked me up and took me to this office. First thing they tell me is that I'm going to play receiver. Now, when I stepped into that office, I'd never had a conversation with white people before. The general manager, the director of personnel, they have these white shirts and ties. Coming from the South, I didn't look anybody in the eye. I looked down at the floor. They said they needed me to sign this contract. If I didn't, I was going to have to go to Canada. I wasn't going to get any more money, they said. My coach was asking for too much. They've got the papers out, the pen. What do I do now? I tell them I need to call my mama. They said go ahead. I called Coach. I don't know what he told them, but they backed down. We eventually got that thing up to about an $8,000 bonus and a $15,000 salary.

Jerry Izenberg: Eddie and I were on the phone that day. This is when Eddie decided James was going to have problems. They brought him in for an early camp, and, according to Eddie, they had three quarterbacks. The first two lived at a hotel, and James was in the YMCA.

James Harris: They took me to my room. Had me staying at the YMCA for six dollars a night. When O.J. came to town, he was staying in a suite at the Hilton. They gave me a job, working in the equipment room, putting laces in shoes. I didn't know if this was part of the game or what, but I decided not to tell Coach Robinson about it. I didn't want to put all this pressure on him. He was doing enough.

Marlin Briscoe: Shack and I shared an apartment together. We had a lot of time for conversation about our experiences. You could tell he was very uncomfortable. Everything was new to him. He was so quiet around training camp, people thought he couldn't communicate. All of the blacks on that team—O.J., Max Anderson, and Haven Moses—all of us lived in the same building. When Shack got home, he was completely different. When he got home, he was laughing and joking and telling these funny stories. He was one of the smartest people I ever met. But because of his demeanor, a lot of players in Buffalo didn't see him as a leader—the way they thought a leader should be.

James was not outgoing or gregarious on the field. I think he was trying to watch himself, monitor himself, make sure he did the right things and said the right things. It was completely different for him and me only because of previous cultural experiences, the way we grew up. That was one of the reasons it was so much more difficult for him to make the transition than it was for me.

James Harris: I wouldn't get any work in during practice, but they'd keep two or three of us afterward to throw. That was my time. I was ready for it. Every night, I stayed in and studied. I wasn't going to let them say black quarterbacks were dumb. Then I pulled a muscle in my stomach.

Back in those days, if you got hurt, they were going to cut you. Every day, about five or six in the morning, they'd knock on the doors. You'd hear it down the hall. They'd knock on the door—*bam, bam, bam.* That meant they're cutting you. My room was in the middle. In those days, they cut every day. So you're lying in bed and you hear them skip over your door, and you know you made it another day. You got twenty-four more hours.

Marlin Briscoe: I remember coming to training camp when Jack Kemp was there, and Jack would have to run almost to the sideline to throw the ball, because his arm wasn't what it used to be. Shack would stand in the pocket, and the ball would just rifle down the sideline.

Jack Kemp: Shack was the only quarterback I knew who had a stronger arm than me. He was a tremendous talent, a diamond in the rough. You look at the quarterbacks of today—I was watching Michael Vick and the Falcons play the other day—and Shack Harris was as good as any of them. But at the time, he was undeveloped.

Marlin Briscoe: What hurt him initially was the fact that he was a rookie replacing an icon. When he first got to camp, he was hurt, and then he had some stomach problems that set him back. Jack was hurt. Flores was hurt. That's why they wanted me to throw.

James Harris: I was throwing the ball pretty good in practice, calling Coach Robinson every night for advice. Before a preseason game in Detroit, Coach Rauch tells me I'll be playing the second half. Well, in those days, you called your own plays, and having to go into the huddle and call plays was rough, you know? I realized if I play bad, I'm going home, and if I play good, I may still go home. That's what's going through your mind.

I called Coach. He says, "Get your five passes and your five runs, okay? Make sure you know them. If they send something in from the bench and you're not sure what it is, stay with one of your five passes." The other thing he told me was to get the ball to O.J. as many times as you can. So I go to Detroit with my five passes and my five runs. I'm not concerned about getting cut anymore. I don't take that to the game with me. I'm more concerned about not making mistakes.

I couldn't read coverages—I didn't know all the reads—so I read receivers. If I thought there was enough space, I threw a fastball as soon as the receiver turned, just like in sandlot. I threw into coverages and everything. Maybe I wasn't throwing to the right guy, but I was hitting the targets.

Marlin Briscoe: We were down in Birmingham, Alabama, to play the Jets in James' first preseason start. Eddie Robinson came to our room, and, man, they got to telling stories and had me crying laughing. I saw another side of him when Coach Robinson came in.

James Harris: Early on, I got sacked. On the sideline, one coach came up to me and said, "The offensive line says the reason they missed their blocks was because they couldn't understand your diction." At that time, I didn't even know what diction was—we didn't use no words like that in Louisiana—but I understood what he meant. What do I do now? Simple: Call every play on one.

Marlin Briscoe: He was fast off the line, but when we'd run sprints, he'd run slow because he didn't want them to say, "Wow, look at his speed!" We used to race after practice—he and I and O.J. We'd run sprints when nobody was around, betting against each other, and Shack was right there. But he didn't want them to discover that he had this quick step.

James Harris: I ended up winning the job. Rookies weren't starting a whole lot in the NFL back then. So to come into the league when there were none making it, that says a lot for the coach, John Rauch, who was willing to play me. Kemp and those guys were helpful too. I think that in some way, they knew what the situation was, and they helped me become a quarterback.

Marlin Briscoe: As soon as I made the team, James asked me if I wanted to room with him. It was a perfect fit, you know? I told him a lot of the things that were going to happen to him. I don't think he really believed it. Once he got on the field, I don't think he thought there were going to be any setbacks. But I knew what was going to happen. Hey, I was a starter, too. I tried to tell him there were going to be bumps—not from a negative standpoint, but from a preparatory standpoint. James always thought I was bitter.

James Harris: Marlin was as bitter a person as I'd ever met. He was right. He deserved another chance to play. But he didn't get it. When we used to talk, Marlin would tell me, "Don't trust them. You can play good, and they're going to cut you anyway. They don't want a black quarterback." Marlin was hurt, and I hurt for Marlin.

Marlin Briscoe: If I was bitter, I'd have folded my chin and gone home. But I continued to work at making the transition. You can't be bitter and focus on doing what you have to do to stay in the game. As time went on, Shack realized what I was telling him was true. We won four games that first year. With O.J. coming in as a rookie, expectations were high, and we didn't fulfill those expectations. We had a lot of talent, but we weren't very organized. We had a lot of players in the last years of their careers. The mix wasn't good. The blame always goes to the quarterback. When the media talked to him, it wasn't like they got all of these great quotes. If they had interviewed him in my apartment, they would have gotten some great lines. But when they interviewed him on the field, James had to watch every word he said.

The Bills selected another quarterback, San Diego State's Dennis Shaw, in the 1970 draft. In Harris' second preseason, he tore ligaments in his knee and was cut by the Bills, but later re-signed.

James Harris: They cut me in training camp. I read about it in the paper. In those days, they could cut you and bring you back, but I didn't know that. I left, went home to my apartment in Buffalo. I'm home, watching the news, and I hear I'm missing. Next thing I know, Marlin's knocking on the door. Marlin was hot. He could feel my pain. When he heard the news, he drove all the way from Niagara Falls to see me.

Marlin Briscoe: When he got cut, I walked out of camp as a show of solidarity. I shouldn't have. I mean, I could have gotten in real trouble, but I was stubborn in my allegiance to James. I kind of just snuck out of camp because I knew he was down. He was really down. We got something to eat. And talked. The things that had happened to him were the things I told him would happen. I kind of prepared him for them, I think.

James Harris: You dream about playing in the NFL. But if you dream of playing quarterback, it becomes a nightmare.

Marlin Briscoe: James got death threats and negative publicity. The press was always fair to me. When I didn't have a good game, they weren't overly harsh. They were critical, but when I had good games, they gave me kudos. I just felt comfortable playing in Denver. Buffalo was more of a melting pot. You had ethnic groups bumping up against one another. So it was tougher for James.

Doug Williams: With all the things he went through as a quarterback in Buffalo, not one time did Shack mention how tough it was. He didn't want me thinking I couldn't do it because I was black. He used to say, "Hey, cat, if you can throw at Grambling, you can throw anywhere."

By 1971, under new coach Harvey Johnson, the team lost its first ten games behind a poor offensive line. Neither Bills quarterback excelled, but Shaw got a much longer look than Harris. In 1972, with yet another new coach—Briscoe's nemesis, Lou Saban—at the helm, Harris was out of Buffalo's plans.

James Harris: I was struggling, probably holding the ball too long because I didn't want to make a mistake. I knew if I had a bad game that was the end of it. The team wasn't strong at that point. Dennis Shaw threw four interceptions in one game. I was reading all the time that the Bills might go get another quarterback. Lou Saban called me into his office and told me he just couldn't have two young quarterbacks. He released me.

I'd spent the previous off-season working for the Department of Commerce in Washington so I called them and they said they'd give me a job. I drove from Buffalo to DC and went to work and waited to see if another NFL team was going to call. The phone never rang. I was working out every day, watching games on Sunday, but nothing happened. The phone never rang. I had to move on. But Tank Younger, one of the all-time greats at Grambling, was working for the Rams, and he went to the people there and told them to give me a chance. I was rusty, but I did okay. Tank made such a strong pitch that they put me on the practice squad. I had some good days, got back in the groove. And then Chuck Knox came in.

Knox, a former assistant to Weeb Ewbank with the Jets, transformed the Rams into a perennial playoff contender. In 1973, the team's quarterback was the aging John Hadl. But Harris' skill was evident, and as his confidence grew, so did his claim to the starting job. In 1974, Hadl was traded to Green Bay, and Harris started eleven games and threw eleven touchdown passes (scoring five more on foot) to lead the Rams to the NFC championship game. The man from Monroe was selected to the Pro Bowl team.

Tom Mack, former Rams offensive lineman: Ron Jaworski was clearly the guy they wanted to back up John Hadl, but he got hurt in a weird way. We were playing in Atlanta, and we went out, had some drinks, and stopped for some hamburgers. Jaworski was sitting in the front seat of this cab with his arm in back of the seat and his hand around the post between the front and back door. One of the guys got out of the car and slammed the door on his hand, crushed the end of the right index finger on his passing hand. He ended up in the emergency room in the middle of the night. They were lucky to save the tip of his finger. Harris stepped in and performed right away.

Skip Bayless, former *LA Times* sportswriter: He could rise completely above the game because his arm was so big and he was a ballerina in the pocket. He could really move around for a guy who was six-four.

Fred Dryer, former NFL defensive lineman: He led the team on the field and off. He was great in the locker room and, as we used to joke, on the back of the bus. People would rally around James.

Tom Mack: James Harris clearly stepped up in terms of his ability to execute and to command real respect in the huddle. He not only understood what the play was, but he embraced it and knew he could execute it. And that confidence translated to everybody feeling like, Hey, this is right. We've got the right people, and we've got the right team. We can make this play.

Harold Jackson: I admired the way he stood in the pocket and threw the ball. You run a shallow crossing route with a shorter quarterback, and the ball comes at you like it's leaving a tunnel. It surprises you. But James Harris stood like a pole, as tall as the offensive line, so his ball was very easy to catch. Everybody says he threw hard, but he didn't. He had great touch on his ball. He threw the go route, the fade route, and the comeback—one of the toughest routes to throw—better than anybody I played with. The ball was right up on me by the time I made my break. He called me Hands and I called him Sugar Shack. He never would tell nobody where Shack came from. We're still trying to find out.

James Harris: My father and brother were named Nashall. N-A-S-H-A-L-L. But a lot of people couldn't pronounce that so they used to call him Mashak, like in the Bible, Mashak and the billygoat. In the South, everybody had a nickname. My brother became Shack. I became Little Shack. When my brother left for the Army, guys just called me Shack.

Tom Mack: In the NFC championship game in Minnesota in 1974, James Harris was scrambling on a pass play, and he threw the ball downfield to Harold Jackson inside the five yard line. Tommy Bell was an official in that game. He turned to lineman Joe Scibelli and me, looks at us in amazement, and says, "I think that's the best play I've ever seen a quarterback make."

James Harris: I hit Harold Jackson, and he took it to the two yard line in the third quarter. We quarterback sneak. I went with a little longer count, and we get called for a false start. Now we're on the seven and Minnesota is a good goal-line team. They stopped us. On third down, I tried to spread the defense out, but my pass was tipped, and they picked it off. We missed out on the opportunity to go to the Super Bowl right there. The Vikings won 14–10. There are three or four games in my career I think about all the time. That Minnesota game is one of them. I'm still trying to figure out a way to win it.

Jerry Izenberg: James Harris would have been the first black quarterback in the Super Bowl if Tom Mack had not jumped offside. They were on the two yard line. I mean, shit, that cost them the game.

Tom Mack: I didn't move. Alan Page jumped offside, and the umpire initially called the penalty on him, but the line judge comes in and says, "Somebody must have moved on the inside." It was a bad call. They get a tipped ball interception, and we get nothing. It was just crazy.

James Harris: In 1974, I'm number one or two in the league in passing, MVP of the Pro Bowl. The next year, I hurt my shoulder and Jaworski plays some. I hurt my shoulder again at the end of the season, Jaworski plays, and we win. Now we have a playoff game against St. Louis. Coach Knox says if I practice, he's going to play me. So I practiced. During warm-ups, he tells me it doesn't look like it's working. He's going to start Jaworski. I was not happy with that. I'd played with a sore arm all season. Jaworski wins. Now I'm getting all kinds of hate mail. Next game—another NFC championship game—Coach says he's going with me. My shoulder was feeling better, but not a hundred percent. My first pass gets picked off. Coach Knox benched me right there. Jaworski was a really good player, but he didn't get us the win. Now the owner Carroll Rosenbloom is upset, and I'm getting even more hate mail.

Tom Mack: With quarterbacks, Carroll Rosenbloom's feeling was that if you didn't win, get somebody else. With John Hadl, we had the best record in football in 1973. He's the MVP, and logic tells you to keep him for one more year and win the championship. But they trade him for two or three first-round draft choices because they think the team's so good. Well, to some extent that's true, but you put yourself at a disadvantage no matter how good your replacement is.

THE FIRST STRING

As any black quarterback will tell you, it takes more than brains and muscle to defeat a hundred years of discrimination. These ten mavericks put their hearts into the cause.

FREDERICK DOUGLASS "FRITZ" POLLARD

First
AFRICAN-AMERICAN SIGNAL-CALLER
1894-1986

Hometown Chicago
College Brown University (1915-18)
Career Akron Pros (1919-21), Milwaukee Badgers (1922), Hammond Pros (1923), Gilberton Cadamounts (1923-24), Hammond Pros (1925), Akron Indians (1925), Providence Steam Roller (1925), Akron Indians (1926)
Also First African-American coach in professional football

WILLIE THROWER

First
**AFRICAN-AMERICAN QUARTERBACK
TO THROW A PASS IN THE NFL**
1930-2002

Hometown New Kensington, Pennsylvania
College Michigan State (1949-52)
Career Chicago Bears (1953), Winnipeg Blue Bombers (1954-56)

GEORGE TALIAFERRO

First
AFRICAN-AMERICAN QUARTERBACK SELECTED IN THE NFL DRAFT
1927-

Hometown Gates, Tennessee
College Indiana University (1945, 1947-48)
Career Los Angeles Dons (1949), New York Yanks (1950-51), Dallas Texans (1952), Baltimore Colts (1953-54), Philadelphia Eagles (1955)

SANDY STEPHENS

First
AFRICAN-AMERICAN QUARTERBACK TO LEAD A DIVISION I-A TEAM TO A NATIONAL CHAMPIONSHIP
1940-2000

Hometown Uniontown, Pennsylvania
College University of Minnesota (1959-61)
Career Montreal Alouettes (1962), Toronto Argonauts (1963)

MARLIN BRISCOE

First — AFRICAN-AMERICAN TO START AT QUARTERBACK IN THE AFL
1945-

Hometown Omaha, Nebraska
College University of Omaha (1963-67)
Career Denver Broncos (1968), Buffalo Bills (1969-71), Miami Dolphins (1972-74), San Diego Chargers (1975), Detroit Lions (1975), New England Patriots (1976)

JAMES HARRIS

First AFRICAN-AMERICAN QUARTERBACK TO LEAD AN NFL TEAM TO THE PLAYOFFS
1947-

Hometown Monroe, Louisiana
College Grambling State (1965-68)
Career Buffalo Bills (1969-71), Los Angeles Rams (1973-76), San Diego Chargers (1977-79)
Also First African-American to open an NFL season at quarterback; first African-American quarterback to play in the Pro Bowl

DOUG WILLIAMS

 **AFRICAN-AMERICAN QUARTERBACK TO WIN THE SUPER BOWL**
1955-

Hometown Zachary, Louisiana
College Grambling State (1974-77)
Career Tampa Bay Buccaneers (1978-82), Oklahoma Outlaws (1984-85), Washington Redskins (1986-89)

DONOVAN McNABB

First **AFRICAN-AMERICAN QUARTERBACK TO SIGN A $100 MILLION CONTRACT**
1976-

Hometown Chicago
College Syracuse University (1995-98)
Career Philadelphia Eagles (1999-present)

MICHAEL VICK

First AFRICAN-AMERICAN QUARTERBACK
SELECTED NO. 1 IN THE NFL DRAFT
1980-

Hometown Newport News, Virginia
College Virginia Tech (1999-2000)
Career Atlanta Falcons (2001-present)

WARREN MOON

AFRICAN-AMERICAN QUARTERBACK INDUCTED INTO THE HALL OF FAME
1956-

Hometown Los Angeles
College University of Washington (1975-77)
Career Edmonton Eskimos (1978-83), Houston Oilers (1984-93), Minnesota Vikings (1994-96), Seattle Seahawks (1997-98), Kansas City Chiefs (1999-2000)

Fred Dryer: James was underestimated by the coaching staff—not because he was black, but because Chuck Knox's philosophy of football would never empower a quarterback. He didn't want a quarterback to call the plays. It was Chuck's playcalling on the sideline that ruled the day.

Tom Mack: You have two really good years, and all of a sudden, you're chopped liver. You feel like they're dealing you off the bottom of the deck. That must have been tough on him.

James Harris: After the '75 season, Carroll Rosenbloom indicated that he wanted Jaworski to start, but they draft Pat Haden out of USC. So there's all this talk about the quarterback position. I always thought, if you're the starter, you have to lose the job in training camp, right? Well, we get to camp and they're rotating the three of us. Rosenbloom calls Jaworski and wants to sign him to a new contract, but because of the way things are going, Jaworski doesn't know what to do. And then everything becomes clear.

Harold Jackson: We looked up to Shack as our leader, the guy who could get us over the hump. We always had a team meeting in the morning. Chuck Knox would come and talk to us. I'll never forget that day when defensive coordinator Ray Malavasi shows up instead, says, "Okay, break up." We knew something was going on. We found out later that Rosenbloom wanted Knox to start Pat Haden. Chuck Knox was really sick about that. James Harris took us all the way to the playoffs.

Brad Pye Jr., former sports editor, *Los Angeles Sentinel*: I still believe Chuck Knox wanted to play James Harris. When Jim Hart of the St. Louis Cardinals got hurt after he was invited to play in the 1975 Pro Bowl, Knox [who coached the NFC team that year] brought in Harris as a substitute and he ended up as the game's MVP. So Chuck wanted to play Harris, but his hands were tied.

Harold Jackson: Here we were playing the Vikings in Minnesota in the 1976 NFC championship game, and we're down on the one-yard line. We have James Harris—six-four, about 215 pounds—and all he has to do is fall forward and he's in the end zone. But he's on the sideline. They tried the sneak with Pat Haden and the Vikings stood him straight up. We had to kick a field goal and they blocked it and took it ninety yards for a touchdown. They beat us.

Fred Dryer: During the seventies, the Rams were always in championship games. But their one area of inconsistency was quarterback. I've got team photographs from the years I played there. Every single year, there was a different quarterback. Why couldn't the organization pick one and keep him there? I was always surprised they didn't stick with James Harris. I know he got hurt, but they all get hurt. I think it was just the neurotic behavior of Carroll Rosenbloom and general manager Don Klosterman putting pressure on Chuck Knox's run-type offense.

The Rams had a proud tradition of quarterback controversies going back for decades, and Harris was embroiled in several—first with Hadl, then with Ron Jaworski, and later with Pat Haden—before leaving the club following the 1976 season. But there was also a special stigma attached to being a black quarterback, even in Los Angeles.

James Harris: Jaworski and I were roommates at the Beverly Hilton the night before one game. When I came through the doors at about six o'clock, people were standing around the lobby. The staff eased me aside and told me the hotel had received some calls—death threats. They added some security and had someone take me to my room. They had guards outside the door. The next morning, Jaworski tells me, "Maybe we ought to ride in separate cars, 'cause one of us has to make sure we get to the game!"

Down on the field, they had light security around the bench. I'm trying not to worry about it. But every once in a while you start looking around and panicking. You look at the crowd and it hits you. When you go back in the game, you just got to tell yourself, Hey, what can you do?

One day, the police come to practice. Everybody's trying to figure out why they're there. After practice, they call me over, say I beat up some man late last night. I told them it wasn't me, I wasn't even there, but they said they had witnesses. One of the coaches comes over and says he saw me come in for curfew before eleven o'clock that night. They didn't arrest me, but they said they were going to do some further investigating. Later, somebody called me up and said, "I just want you to know that I'm a fan of yours and I saw you beat that man up." I said, "You didn't see me!"

A couple of times after that, I was pulled over by the police. Now I'm thinking that I'm being targeted. A cop on a motorcycle tails me, so I pull over. It's dark. He jumps at the window with his gun out, says, "Put your hands up!" I try to explain, but he takes me in and locks me up. Some other cops recognized me and said I'm not the guy they were looking for.

The second time, I didn't pull over right away, because it was so dark. I drove to the next exit and pulled over in a lighted area. They had cops everywhere. The guy tailing me had radioed for backup. Once again they recognized me, but still put me in a holding cell. There was a guy in LA with the same name, same height, same car, same birthday. He had numerous arrests. Only thing different was our Social Security numbers. I wasn't convinced that was true. I thought maybe all those things were connected.

After the 1976 season, Ron Jaworski was traded to the Philadelphia Eagles. He later steered them to the Super Bowl, where they lost to the Raiders 27–10. Harris was traded to the San Diego Chargers, where he played three more seasons before retiring.

James Harris: When the '76 season ended, I was so tired. Mentally tired. I wasn't sure I wanted to play anymore. I was the guy who worked out during the off-season, but I just couldn't get myself ready for the job. I lost my passion. Coach Knox was supportive, but the owner was going over his head. There was nothing I could do. I'd been through this so many times—the racism, the hate mail. Like anybody else, I wanted to excel in the game. I wanted to be recognized. When I left Los Angeles, I understood I was leaving behind any desire for recognition. Whatever I had accomplished, I left behind. It hasn't been important since. When I was a teenager, most quarterbacks were making money doing appearances. I ain't never made no money. Nobody even asked me for an autograph. Most of the young quarterbacks don't know the story. The young quarterbacks, they're making money at autograph signings. I've never done none of that. I've never even been invited back to Buffalo.

I went to San Diego because I knew I'd learn a lot about the game—especially the passing game—from Don Coryell, and I wanted to coach. But when I got out of the game, nobody would have me. I couldn't get nothing, not even a college job. At that time, it was a closed system, and I knew it. They told me I needed to coach at a high school.

Coach Ray Perkins gave me a scouting job down in Tampa. But the money wasn't enough to live on in LA. I had to borrow money to survive. I didn't tell nobody about my financial situation. I didn't share that with people. If I was going to make it, I had to roll up my sleeves and do the dirty work. I just had to go out there and get it done.

Skip Bayless: To this day, I admire what Shack Harris did in Los Angeles, because he was a very sensitive and tortured soul. He got caught in a cross fire with about four quarterbacks: John Hadl, Ron Jaworski, Pat Haden, and Joe Namath. He was constantly looking over his shoulder, to the point of becoming a little paranoid. He didn't get enough credit for laying the groundwork. He was putting too much pressure on his own shoulder pads, because of the burden of color. I don't know that any quarterback has had to look over his shoulder as much as James did.

Fred Dryer: James was the right guy, a great leader. He had the skills to be a championship quarterback. He was on the wrong team at the wrong time.

Warren Moon, 1977.

CHAPTER SIX

WANTED MAN

As the NFL continued to halt the dreams of black quarterbacks, many African-Americans turned north to the Canadian Football League. Between 1960 and 1980, dozens demonstrated their ability to lead and win without so much as a nod from the scouts in their homeland. And then came Warren Moon, the first to show that the road to Canada could lead to the Pro Football Hall of Fame.

Warren Moon: Growing up in L.A., I was a huge Rams fan. I rooted for whoever was playing QB for them, starting with Roman Gabriel. That's the earliest I remember—Gabriel, James Harris, and the black backup, John Walton. Me and my friends would wait outside the locker room at the Coliseum and watch the players come out. I was too shy to ask for an autograph. I waited just to see them in real life. The Rams seemed to be more open-minded about quarterbacks than other franchises. I thought, "Okay, there might be an opportunity to play this position one day."

Moon began playing football in 1967 at age 11 in the Pee Wee division of the Baldwin Hills Pop Warner Football Association. Though originally a running back and a linebacker, his precocious arm and his leadership skills quickly emerged. In three of his four years in Pop Warner, Moon played quarterback.

Warren Moon: I was going to go to Arizona State. They were recruiting me as a QB, but, all of a sudden, two top quarterbacks committed to Arizona State. The coach came back and said, "We still want to sign you, but we want you to play defensive back." I said, "No thank you."

My high school coach, Jack Epstein, was leaving to become the offensive coordinator at West Los Angeles Junior College. He thought playing there could improve my odds. A year later, USC expressed interest in me. John McKay had a history of playing black quarterbacks, and Vince Evans was playing there, but I didn't want to redshirt. Cal was a classy, drop-back school, and I wanted to play in that style of offense, but they ended up going with a kid named Joe Roth. I wasn't interested in UCLA. They were running the option, and I didn't want to be labeled a running quarterback. I wanted to go somewhere where I could throw the ball.

So it came down to Washington and Colorado. I really wanted to be on the West Coast, relatively close to my family. I wanted to play in the Pac-8. It was a dream of mine to some day play in the Rose Bowl.

Washington had a black quarterback, Cliff McBride. He told me not to come there because he didn't think I'd get a chance to play. I'd heard about prior racial tensions in the program. They had to bring in an African-American assistant athletic director, a guy named Don Smith, to clean it up.

In the end, I chose Washington. My first two years there were tough. Don James was rebuilding the program. His philosophy was sound, physical football. We became a conservative, ball-control team, so I didn't throw the way I wanted to. We opened my senior year 1–1, then got beat by Syracuse on a last-second field goal. But we got things turned around and earned a trip to the Rose Bowl against Michigan. We were huge underdogs.

A few days before the game, both teams toured Disneyland. It was a PR thing. I remembered seeing photos of the game's starting quarterbacks in front of Disneyland every year in the papers. For some reason, Rick Leach of Michigan decided not to be in the picture in 1978; they paired me with Michigan's All-America center instead. My teammates were really insulted by that. We used it as motivation. I later discovered that Leach didn't want to take the picture because he had been to an Orange Bowl and a Rose Bowl, didn't play very well, and felt he got too caught up in the promotional stuff. He wanted to stay in the background.

We ended up beating them, 27–20. It's still one of the most exhilarating moments of my career—winning The Granddaddy of Them All in front of 106,000 people. I thought it was going to catapult me into the NFL.

Leigh Steinberg, Moon's agent: I met Warren fresh out of the Rose Bowl, and his maturity was evident immediately. He had not been treated well at Washington. The abuse he took from the fans was extraordinary. But he never expressed bitterness. He didn't lash out. He talked to me about thirty times before selecting me. He had me vetted with prominent alums, even a football writer from the *L.A. Times*. I could have been confirmed for Secretary of State when it was all over. That's when I realized I was dealing with a unique personality.

Warren Moon: I got a lot of praise on the banquet circuit and played in the Challenge Bowl, where coaches and scouts looked at me. But the attention stopped after that. I didn't have anybody coming out to do personal workouts. I wasn't invited to the combine. I was pissed. Player of the Year in the Pac-8, MVP of the Rose Bowl—what more do you want?

Roy S. Johnson: It was racism, pure and simple. No matter how much success he had in college, no matter that he was the MVP of the biggest bowl game—the granddaddy of all bowl games—he was still not perceived as capable of performing at that level in the NFL.

Brad Pye Jr.: He should have been drafted, no question about it. He was a better quarterback than Pat Haden. They both played in the Pac-8. Warren Moon had the wrong paint job. That's why he didn't get drafted.

Leigh Steinberg: The interest in him was far less than his physical skills and his character demanded. He should have been a franchise quarterback, but there were doubts. In college, Warren had played as a roll-out quarterback. His success had primarily come in his senior year. Teams were asking if he'd be willing to change positions.

Warren said, "Never. No one's ever going to get me to forsake my dream. I was born to be a quarterback."

Warren Moon: And then the Canadian Football League started knocking on my door.

The opportunities denied to black quarterbacks in the States were being offered in Canada, to the likes of Chuck Ealey, who turned down a scholarship offer to play third-string at Miami of Ohio and instead steered the University of Toledo to thirty-five straight wins, and Condredge Holloway, an All-America player at Tennessee who passed for 3,102 yards and was the MVP in the 1975 Hula Bowl. J.C. Watts, who led the Oklahoma Sooners to two consecutive Orange Bowl victories, followed in 1981. Danny Barrett, University of Cincinnati star (who would set the CFL record for most passing yards in a single game at 601), arrived soon thereafter. The wide-open style of play promoted by the CFL was ideally suited to the diverse talents of quarterbacks who were mobile.

J.C. Watts: In Canada, people were more accepting. At one time, seven of the league's nine starting quarterbacks were black. When I first went to Canada, there was even a black head coach—Willie Wood of Toronto.

Chuck Ealey: There was no racial bias at all. They wanted the best athletes they could get.

Danny Barrett: It's a diverse country. They didn't have the same racial tensions—not to the degree you had in the U.S. In Canada, they just enjoyed the game. That's why so many guys came. They didn't want to go through the aggravation.

J.C. Watts: The rules are very different. Three downs, twelve men to a side, everybody going in motion, even toward the line of scrimmage. Certain positions were designated for Americans and certain positions for Canadians. Canadians played on the offensive line and Americans played on the defensive line. The Americans started playing football in the fifth or sixth grade. Canadians didn't start until high school. The quarterback suffered the consequences. When you ran, you ran out of necessity.

Condredge Holloway: You have to get ten yards in two downs and there aren't many running backs who average five yards a carry.

Warren Moon: Hugh Campbell, the coach of the Edmonton Eskimos, came down to visit me and we spent three hours watching film, talking X's and O's. They brought me up to Edmonton to show me around, but every day, in the back of my mind, I was hoping somebody from the NFL was going to call, somebody was going to give me some good news. I'm up visiting Edmonton. There's snow everywhere, but the people are welcoming. And they're offering me the money of a second-round NFL draft pick. They're making it tough for me to say no.

Leigh Steinberg: The Eskimos were a well-run franchise, and Warren's personality didn't lend itself to waiting in tutelage for a number of years; he's got a very strong leadership streak. In Edmonton, he was going to get a chance to prove himself.

Norman H. Kimball, general manager, Edmonton Eskimos: We signed him six weeks before the NFL draft. It was possible the NFL was going to draft him, but there was a lot of indecision. Was I surprised? A bit. Somebody should have taken a shot with him.

Tony Dungy: During pregame warmups, I'd see quarterbacks, especially the backups, throw these bad balls, and I'd think, "How is Warren Moon not playing in the NFL?" It was ludicrous.

Doug Williams: Here's a guy who went to a major university, played against major competition, and put up major numbers, and he didn't get drafted. What's wrong with that picture? It blew my mind.

Warren Moon: Edmonton's season started a lot earlier than the NFL's. Leigh said if I was going to sign with them, do it now—maybe then no one in the NFL would draft me and I could come back as a free agent. That's one reason I signed when I did. On draft day, I had my fingers crossed, hoping nobody picked me.

Leigh Steinberg: Warren got a $35,000 signing bonus and a three-year contract: $35,000, $45,000, $55,000, if I recall correctly. The Eskimos had a quarterback, Tom Wilkinson, but they were very explicit about how Warren was going to end up, in essence, the starting quarterback. True to their word, for Warren's first two years, they pulled Wilkinson very quickly.

Norman H. Kimball: Whenever Warren got on the field, he took advantage of the opportunity almost instantly.

Tom Wilkinson: In the Rose Bowl, I saw a quarterback with a strong arm who could put touch on the ball, who could run, and who could throw on the run. I thought, "There's a guy who's going to be in the NFL next year." He had the height, he had the arm, he had everything. A couple of months later, he shows up in Edmonton. *Edmonton?* It was a surprise.

After seeing him in person, there was no question in my mind, he was as good as I had thought. In fact, he was better. The CFL allowed only two American quarterbacks per team, and there were already two of us on the Eskimos—Bruce Lemmerman and me. Together, we had gone to four Grey Cups in five years. I knew one of us was going to get cut. I went from 212 pounds to about 170 to compete. I knew I had to be in great shape, maybe the best shape of my life.

Warren Moon: Canada was like a finishing school for black quarterbacks. We all looked at it as an opportunity to play and get better every week, figuring maybe somebody would see us and like us. There's more passing in the CFL—a lot more passing. The offense is much more aggressive because you only have three downs. And, because of the wider field, you have to be more versatile. You've got to be able to throw it from the drop-back, but you've also got to be able to throw on the run.

Tom Wilkinson: He was a great student of the game. We had this play I kept trying in practice, a play-action with motion—the slot-back and running back on the play-side hitting the line at almost the same time, the outside receiver running a post. It never, ever worked. Warren went into his first exhibition game and ran the play five times. It worked every time. This was a kid who was around for just four weeks. I mean, he was a natural. In a playoff game my last year, going into a very strong wind, Warren rolled to his left, which is the hardest thing for a right-handed quarterback to do. He just flipped his wrist and the ball went forty-five yards on a line to Brian Kelly for a touchdown. I'm not kidding. It was one of the most unbelievable passes I've ever seen.

Leigh Steinberg: He had a magnificent supporting cast in Edmonton: running back Jim Germany, receivers Waddell Smith and Brian Kelly. It was a very talented group. Hugh Campbell was a superb coach. And they had a very strong general manager in Norm Kimball. They won Grey Cup after Grey Cup after Grey Cup.

Skip Bayless: Warren Moon didn't just go to Canada—he owned Canada.

Warren Moon: There were NFL scouts watching players up there, but my big break came when the NFL went on strike in 1982 and they showed three or four of our games on NBC. I got showcased on national TV. And when we won five championships, I'm sure that opened people's eyes. If I was just a good quarterback who won one or two Grey Cups, they wouldn't have wanted me in the NFL. I had to have exceptional ability.

Playing in Edmonton was one of the most positive experiences in my life. I'm sure there are racist people up there, but I never heard anything. I felt like I was judged on how I played. At times, I thought I'd stay there for the rest of my career. But there were days when it was so cold at practice, I started wondering, "What the hell am I doing here? Why am I not playing in the United States?" I was looking at guys in the NFL and thinking, "I'm better than them."

In six seasons with the Edmonton Eskimos, Moon threw for 21,228 yards and 144 touchdowns, and NFL scouts began to take a second look.

Leigh Steinberg: He really enjoyed the experience, but there was a sadness, a yearning. When we went to watch the Super Bowl, he was like a kid with his nose pressed up against the window. His dream was to play in the NFL, and he knew he was good enough to do it.

Gene Upshaw: Look at the yards, look what he did. They can try to discount the stuff he did in Canada. But guess what? He still threw that ball. They still caught it. And they still won.

Warren Moon: It was burning inside me. I had to prove to myself that I could play against the best, and the best players were in the National Football League.

Leigh Steinberg: Warren was making significant money. At that point, the financial disparity between the two leagues was not what it is today. CFL teams were able to put together competitive packages for players like Vince Ferragamo and Tom Cousineau. Warren also had endorsement deals. We started with a two-year contract, replaced it with a ten-year contract, then modified the ten to two, for 1982 and 1983. With quarterbacks, you have less nasty contract fights because people need happy quarterbacks.

Hugh Campbell and Norm Kimball understood that Warren had given them six extraordinary years. They didn't want to stand in the way of his dreams. Warren had been carefully calibrating the progression of his career. Knowing that the USFL was coming, we set the stage for 1984—provoking a three-league fight for his services.

Warren Moon: My marketability was as high as it was going to get. A lot of people don't know this, but the Oilers flew me down to tour their facilities in 1983, a year before my Edmonton contract was up. They snuck me into town and took me to dinner, showed me around when nobody was there—this whole secret visit. But I could not get out of my contract just yet. The following year, Houston came back, of course—along with everybody else.

Leigh Steinberg: About twelve NFL teams expressed interest in him, as well as a couple in the CFL and several in the USFL. Warren wanted to meet with all of them, so we set out on this whirlwind tour. He visited Houston, and Bud Adams joked with him about the oil fields he could own. He went to New Orleans, and John Mecom took him out on a boat. He said, "This skyline could be all yours one day." Hugh Culverhouse asked him, "How would you like to own the Tampasphere?" When he got to New York, the back page of the *Post* read "Spaced Out Jints Shoot the Moon" in a big, bold headline. It was that way everywhere.

Warren Moon: When Leigh does negotiations, he throws out numbers and quotes that stick. Things like, "I think this kid is going to be the highest paid player in the league." You say that in enough interviews and it sets the tone.

Leigh Steinberg: The furor started to build and build. There were so many cities interested in him, it became a national story. Everywhere we went, I kept saying he was going to be the highest paid player in history. Now, the market was untested. Free agency didn't surface until 1993. And, as the economics went up, teams dropped out. Warren narrowed it down to Houston and Seattle. Both ended up offering $5.5 million over five years—the largest NFL contract in history. But Houston offered a $200,000 salary and a $4.5 million signing bonus, which meant Warren was not only getting the largest bonus of all time, he was effectively getting eighty percent of the contract guaranteed.

Doug Williams: When everybody was courting him, I said, "Damn, I'm making peanuts and they're fixing to pay this guy from Canada a ton of money." I got to the NFL ahead of him and I was barely making it. In my fifth year, I was the fifty-fourth highest paid quarterback in the league and there were only twenty-eight teams. They had backups making more money than me. But then I thought, "They're about to give a black quarterback all this money. That's big time. We've come a long ways, baby."

Warren Moon: The Oilers had also hired Hugh Campbell to be their head coach. But I had a home in Seattle. The Seahawks had a pretty good team. I loved Chuck Knox, Shack Harris' coach with the

Rams. He had a history with black quarterbacks. Chick Harris, who recruited me at Washington, was the running backs coach.

Leigh Steinberg: Warren's heart was heavily in Seattle. Paraphrasing Thomas Wolfe, I pointed out that you can't always go home again. If you're the starting quarterback and things don't go well, it's not the most tranquil, emotionally nurturing experience as my client Jeff George learned in Indianapolis years later.

The night Warren made his decision was excruciating. He was sitting in his home in Redmond, a suburb on the eastern shore of Seattle right next to Kirkland, where the Seahawks have their facility. There were camera crews camped on his front lawn, all these vans with satellite feeds in the street. He had to go out and face the local media, even fans, and make his announcement.

Warren Moon: I decided to go to Houston because I didn't know if I'd ever be a free agent again. I had to take advantage of the opportunity. And Houston reminded me of my college situation. I was going to a rebuilding team. We were trying to turn it into a Super Bowl franchise. Seattle had just gone to the AFC championship. I didn't feel they needed me as much.

Leigh Steinberg: There were real stresses in Houston—high expectations and times when it was harrowing for Warren's wife, Felicia, to sit in the stands with the kids because of the racial comments. Warren never talked about it, but it took a toll.

Warren Moon: I heard more crap on the East Coast than I did down south—places where the fans were right behind the bench, like Giants Stadium or Foxboro. It was always the same stuff: "Nigger!" or "Hey, Moon, chuck that ball like you chuck a watermelon" or "Throw that ball like you throw a spear." Even if I had won the Super Bowl, people would have called me a nigger. I remember walking off the field with guards surrounding me. They'd ask me before the games, "Do you want to know about the threats or do you want to wait until after the game?" I'm like, "Tell me after the game."

Ernest Givins, Houston Oilers wide receiver: The first couple of years, he really didn't have all the weapons in place. I came along in '86. The next year, we got Haywood Jeffires, Alonzo Highsmith, Curtis Duncan. Then Lorenzo White. Later, we picked up Webster Slaughter and Gerald McNeil. We started putting that thing together, and it became a very potent offense.

The receivers—they used to call us "the little guys"—we played with chips on our shoulders. None of us was taller than five-nine until Haywood came along. They had me in the books at 165 pounds, but I probably weighed closer to 155. Everybody was saying that the little guys couldn't last a whole season with all the pounding we'd take. Well, we held our own.

Warren had a chip on his shoulder, too. He wanted to be Warren Moon the quarterback, not Warren Moon the black quarterback. People kept trying to throw him to the wolves, saying he couldn't do it, but he just kept putting up numbers.

Warren was professional at everything he did. He might get upset with you, but he would never disrespect you. Behind closed doors, I was looking for him to yell, curse, throw something, but he didn't do that. He'd just sit down and say, "Look, I know you got talent. You've got to do this and this" or "I want this out of you, understand?" He was a mentor. You listened.

Every time I scored, I'd do my Electric Slide dance in the end zone. First time I did it, Warren came up to me and said, "What *was* that?" I told him it's a release—everybody says we can't get it done, so I've got to release. Warren looked at me and said, "Don't celebrate until you celebrate." I didn't know what he was talking about, so I asked him. He said the reward comes when your peers—not the public—put you in the Pro Bowl. That's when you celebrate.

Much as he did with the Washington Huskies, Moon molded the Oilers into a formidable team. But, try as he might, he never could lift them into the Super Bowl. Year after year, the team's hopes were dashed in the postseason, most notably the 1993 Wildcard game against the Buffalo Bills in what is perhaps the most memorable playoff collapse in NFL history. Led by backup quarterback Frank Reich, the Bills scored thirty-five unanswered second-half points to overcome a thirty-two-point deficit. Moon drove the Oilers to a field goal to push the game into overtime. His season ended with an interception and a thirty-two-yard kick by Buffalo's Steve Christie.

Ernest Givins: In 1993, we got off to a 1–4 start and Warren told us we had to show them what we got. It was up to us to make it happen. That's all he said. We won eleven games in a row. We were the hottest thing in the NFL, everybody is putting up these tremendous numbers, and all the credit goes to Warren.

I was pretty fast. I ran about a 4.2. Haywood ran a 4.3 and Webster Slaughter ran a 4.3. We had guys out there with so much speed, free to do what we thought we should do in the run and shoot, and all the pressure was on Warren. He had to know everything, anticipate when we'd break, how we broke, who was going to run what kind of route. Everything was on Warren.

The playoff losses hurt. Every single time. In the Buffalo game, we played freelance football in the first half. We were up 35–3, and then we stopped playing freelance football. Buffalo caught us off-guard with an on-side kick, and it started going downhill from there. To come back from 35–3? That's unheard of.

Leigh Steinberg: They were snake-bit to lose that game the way they did. It was one of the most humiliating losses in the history of professional football.

Ernest Givins: After the game, Warren said, "We just didn't finish." I said, "C'mon, all this mentor stuff, you gotta come up with something better than that." And he said, "Listen, we didn't finish. Time just ran out on us."

During a stellar seventeen-year NFL career with Houston, Minnesota, Seattle, and Kansas City (he played until age forty-four), Moon accounted for more than 300 touchdowns through the air and on the ground, proving that he was indeed the master of the run and shoot offense. His 49,325 passing yards are the fourth highest total in league history, ranking behind only all-time leader Dan Marino,

Brett Favre, and John Elway. Including his six CFL seasons, Moon's 70,553 passing yards are the most in professional football, some 9,000-plus more than Marino's total.

Donovan McNabb, NFL quarterback: He's the guy I watched when I was growing up. He called me when I was at Syracuse. I talk about it to this day. I was about to hang up on him. I was like, "This isn't a funny joke." We talked for an hour. It was one of the most powerful conversations I've ever had.

Warren Moon: My only regret is not getting to the Super Bowl. There's always that part of you that thinks you haven't done enough. We turned the corner after my third year and were a playoff team for nearly seven years in a row. We just didn't get over that last hurdle.

Doug Williams after winning Super Bowl XXII, 1988.

CHAPTER SEVEN

THE PROMISED
LAND

W hen the Washington Redskins beat the Minnesota Vikings 17–10 in the 1987 NFC championship game, Doug Williams—who hadn't wrested the starting quarterback job from Jay Schroeder until the second half of Washington's regular-season finale—was placed in the position of becoming the first African-American to start under center in a Super Bowl.

Though the historic story line received plenty of attention in the days leading up to the game, Williams' inspiring playoff run was overshadowed by that of his counterpart, Denver's glamour quarterback, John Elway, who, after leading the Broncos to a Super Bowl loss against the Giants a year earlier, seemed ready for his coronation as an all-time great.

The media may have made Elway the headliner, but for those who'd followed or experienced the hard road to glory for black quarterbacks, the game took on an outsize significance, and there could be only one story line: How would Williams react under the pressure? Everyone who sympathized with the plight of the African-American quarterback became a Redskins fan that day.

Roy S. Johnson: There probably isn't an African-American sports fan in America who doesn't remember where he was on that day, just as we remember where we were when Martin Luther King was killed, where we were when the Civil Rights Act was passed.

Joe Greene: I was there as a guest of the Steelers. Obviously I'm an AFC guy, but I pulled so blatantly for Doug, I embarrassed myself—blatantly embarrassed myself.

Randall Cunningham: Oh, I went to that Super Bowl. We had beaten Washington during the regular season. They were our rivals. But as much as I hated that team, I wanted to support Doug. So I called him up and said, "Look, man, I'm coming to check you out!"

Kevin Carroll: I was a Redskins fan that night because of Doug Williams. I'm from Philly. I knew that was blasphemous for an Eagles fan, but other Eagles fans of color were doing it too. We thought maybe that game would be the myth buster. Maybe the time had come when a black quarterback didn't have to be a backup—the last resort.

Doug Williams: John Elway was Denver's quarterback. I was Washington's quarterback. Nobody gave us a chance.

Kevin Carroll: It was all about Elway, the all-American quarterback, Stanford guy. It was like, "Doug Williams? Who's he? Where did he go to school?" The media seemed to feel the story was already written.

Doug Williams: You know what? I probably wasn't given proper due by the media. But that's good in a way, because nobody expected what happened to happen.

George Michael, host, *The Sports Machine*: People didn't give enough credence to how much the players loved Doug. During the strike that year, some teams fell apart. The Redskins had a couple of meetings where Doug brought everybody together. He shut up the bickering. He'd say, "We're not here to argue about the union being right or wrong. We're here to keep the Redskins together. We're gonna come back and win." Everybody rallied around him.

Tom Friend: Washington is a city of power, and the quarterback has the power on a football team. So in Washington, the quarterback carries a lot of weight. People like to say he's a close second to the president. A lot of players have crumbled under that weight. Heath Shuler. Jay Schroeder. There's always a quarterback controversy.

Joe Gibbs liked to have a veteran backup for a young quarterback. Early on, Jay Schroeder was the indisputable starter, the superstar-in-waiting, and Doug was there for insurance. In 1986, Doug threw only one pass. Schroeder played the entire year, took the team to the NFC championship game where they got killed by the Giants 17–0.

In the '87 opener against the Eagles, Jay got hurt. Doug comes out and wins the game. He's the starter going into the strike, but the strike gives Jay a chance to heal. Now, you have to remember that Washington is a very diverse city, a very ethnic city, and you've got a large African-American population. So Doug was very popular. In the locker room, they loved him. Jay was surly back then—young and defensive.

Well, Doug hurt his back. It was Thanksgiving Day 1987. The Redskins had a walk-through practice before this huge game against the Giants, and Doug tweaks his back and starts having spasms. He can't start the game. Schroeder leads them to a victory, 23–19, and the next week, Jay's the starter. I remember Doug in tears—literally in tears doing an interview—just crying because he lost his starting spot. And I'll never forget this, it changed the course of Doug Williams' life: The Redskins make the playoffs, but they have to beat Minnesota on the last day of the season to clinch a better seed and potential homefield advantage. Jay has a bad first half, and in the third quarter, Gibbs pulls him. If he doesn't pull Jay, Jay's the starter in the playoffs and Doug Williams never becomes Doug Williams. But Gibbs pulls Jay, Doug leads the team to victory, and Doug becomes the starter in the playoffs.

Doug Williams: I signed with Washington because Joe Gibbs asked me if I'd be his backup. I told him, "Yeah, I could be the backup." At the time, I didn't have a job. The USFL had folded, and Joe was the only guy who called. I'd known him pretty well. He was the offensive coordinator in Tampa when I got drafted in 1978. I used to spend hours at Joe's house going over stuff when I was a rookie. I used to eat dinner at Joe Gibbs' house. I knew his boys, J.D. and Coy. He's one of the two people most responsible for drafting me. General manager Ken Herock actually lived at Grambling my senior year. During the off-season, Gibbs came down to Louisiana and spent the day while I was student-teaching. He took me and my future wife, Janet, to

McDonald's. That was the Tampa Bay budget at the time. From my understanding, when he got back, Joe told them, "If y'all are looking for a quarterback, y'all need to draft Doug Williams."

Jimmie Giles: Joe Gibbs took Doug under his wing just like he was his son. As far as Tampa head coach John McKay and Joe Gibbs were concerned, color didn't matter. Back in 1970, when McKay was coaching USC, he had a black quarterback named Jimmy Jones and a black running back named Sam "Bam" Cunningham. He went to Alabama and just killed Bear Bryant, changed Bear Bryant's mind about African-American athletes. What did Bear do? He went out and started recruiting black athletes.

Doug Williams: When we went to training camp in Tampa Bay in 1979, we had a boom box in the dressing room. Our theme song was "Ain't No Stopping Us Now." We were 5–0 before we lost our first game. The season before we were 5–11. A lot of people don't realize it, but we were nine points away from the Super Bowl in '79. We played a veteran Rams team in the NFC championship game—Jack Youngblood, Jim Youngblood, Fred Dryer. We probably didn't take them as seriously as we should have. We had beaten them earlier in the season, so we were a little cocky. I tore a biceps muscle early in the game and missed most of the third quarter and all of the fourth quarter. We lost 9–0. I always think about that. If I had played, we could have won.

Jimmie Giles: I remember our center, Steve Wilson, saying once, "It didn't matter if we were down two touchdowns. If Doug Williams was behind me, I knew we had a chance to win." When Doug got hurt

149

against the Rams, it was chaos, because we didn't have a chance. We went to the playoffs three out of five years with him at quarterback, but management didn't want to pay the guy. After his contract was up, the owner, Hugh Culverhouse, wanted to offer him a piece of real estate. He said, it's worth this amount of money now, but it could be worth *this* amount in years to come. If I recall, that piece of property is still sitting there. There's nothing on it but a Wal-Mart. The Buccaneers clearly didn't want him to be the face of the franchise, because he had done everything he was supposed to do. He was a winner. He'd taken our team to the playoffs. If they'd paid Doug $3 million, we would have gone to two Super Bowls.

George Michael: The Thursday before the 1988 game, Doug was beginning to get a little tired because there were so many interviews and so many of them were inane. As he was sitting there in the bleachers, one guy asks him, "How long have you been a black quarterback?" Well, no one really knew what to say. Doug said, "Well, I've been black all my life." I said, "No, Doug, he wants to know how long have you had the brains to be a quarterback?" And everybody laughed. Don't let anyone tell you that that quote was taken out of context, because I was there. We had a camera. The question to him was, quote, "How long have you been a black quarterback?" And the insinuation was, "Well, you're black. How long you been a quarterback, man? That doesn't happen."

Doug Williams: I went for a four-hour root canal the Saturday before the game. I woke up with a toothache—one of those toothaches that gives you a headache. I went to the dentist, and he said, "I'll be honest with you. You're going to have this pain unless we do this root canal." I told him, "Whatever you've got to do." I wasn't thinking about tomorrow—only the pain. That night before the game, I ate a bag full of Hershey's Kisses. That was my routine: Hershey's Kisses before every game. People don't know that. The next morning, I felt no pain. Super Bowl Sunday. Ain't no tomorrow.

Jimmy Raye: When the game started, I had this morbid fear. I did not want him to fail. It's not that I didn't have confidence in his ability; I just thought it was important for him to play well—for the future. So all the kids who were watching and wanted to be quarterbacks would have something to point to, someone who proved it could be done.

Charles Ross: I was worried about the consequences if, say, he threw three interceptions and the Redskins got destroyed. Would all the great stuff he'd done during the regular season be forgotten? Would it have been back to square one for black quarterbacks? Even though he said over and over again that he simply wanted to be judged as a quarterback, I think he understood what was on the line.

Kevin Carroll: I thought if he didn't have any crazy turnovers, everybody would say, "Yeah, he was respectable. We have to honor that. He led the team, and he was respectable." Now winning the game was the big hope, but I just wanted him to have a good showing—to not be embarrassed in any way.

Doug Williams: Running out onto the field Super Bowl Sunday was one of the greatest feelings ever. I knew all the things that had been said and written about black quarterbacks over the years. When they called my name, I thought about the guys that came before me, the James Harrises and the Joe Gilliams.

Dale Hamer, head linesman: Well, the first quarter pretty much belonged to the Broncos, 10–0. I don't know whether the Redskins were trying to establish the run or Doug wasn't throwing well or what, but they didn't do anything the first couple of series.

Tom Friend: The Broncos get a touchdown on their first play on offense. Elway throws a fifty-six-yard bomb to Ricky Nattiel. On their second drive, Elway catches a pass. He hands the ball off to Steve Sewell, and Sewell throws it back to Elway for a twenty-three-yard gain. Rich Karlis kicks a field goal, and the Broncos are up 10–0.

Kevin Carroll: All the ill-fated thoughts I tried to push to the back of my mind were unfolding. It was like, No! No! No! No! No! We're never going to have a black quarterback again. There will never be another one. This will allow them to say, "See? We told you." I felt if he didn't do well, it was going to close the door even more.

Dale Hamer: When the Broncos went up 10–0, referee Bob McElwee's standing there at the goal line, waiting for the next kickoff. I knew he was probably thinking, Oh, here's my big game, my Super Bowl, and it's going to be a rout. So during the time-out, I said, "Don't worry, Bob. The Redskins are better than this. We're going to have a game."

Bob McElwee, referee: Denver scores a touchdown: 7–0. Denver drives, kicks a field goal: 10–0. Denver kicks off, Ricky Sanders catches the ball, and I'm following him right up the center of the field. He gets to the twenty and they hit him, and out comes the football. Bam! There's a big pile. So umpire Al Conway and I go in there, and we dig the football out. When we get to the bottom—who knows what happened before that—Washington has the ball. I often wonder, with the way the game started, if the Broncos had gotten that football and Elway, great as he was, had put it in the end zone, would things have been different? Nobody will ever know. Because from that play on, Washington just beat their tails off.

Tom Friend: There was so much pressure on him. If he lays an egg, it's a huge step back. And he started off poorly. The team was struggling. When he hurt his knee, it was like the perfect out; here comes Jay Schroeder. But Doug was not going to let Schroeder back on that field.

Doug Williams: Part of the field had just been resodded—a part that didn't get a lot of sun. When I went back and planted, the grass slid out from under my foot. I hyperextended my knee. Unbearable pain. But mentally, *Shoot, I just went through a root canal.* I got up. I wanted to tell the trainer, "Don't touch me."

George Michael: I was sick to my stomach when I saw that. I thought, Man, this guy has worked so hard to get here, and now this? There was this genuine fear that things were not going to work out. He's lying on the field in great pain. They have to help him off, and you figure it's torn ligaments.

Tom Friend: You have to understand, Jay was very unpopular on that team. And in the 1986 NFC championship game against the Giants, Jay was knocked silly by the Giants—L.T. and those guys—and he looked like he was losing it. And Gibbs sent Doug onto the field, and Jay waved him off. As far as Doug was concerned, that was a sign of disrespect. He was disrespected in front of the whole world. Doug never forgot that.

Doug Williams: We were playing against the Giants in a championship game, and Jay took a hard blow. Joe Gibbs sent me into the game. On my way out to the huddle, Jay waved me off the field. It was one of the most embarrassing moments of my life. Like they always say, payback is a mother. That was my payback. He wasn't going to play no more—not if I could help it.

Jimmie Giles: That gave Doug all the willpower in the world to come back. He could not walk the next day. We had to help him down the stairs, help him out of bed. But he was not going to be denied his glory in that game.

Roy S. Johnson: There's a story about Eddie Robinson, sitting in the stands. He had never really challenged his God before, but he looked up at the sky and said, "I know, God, you didn't bring me this far for this to happen." And sure enough, Doug Williams came back into the game after missing just two plays.

Gene Upshaw: I'm sitting in the end zone behind him, and I see him come limping back out, basically dragging his leg.

Kevin Carroll: I was shouting, "Willis Reed! Willis Reed!" My kids were like, "What are you talking about?" I said, "One of the great moments in sports history! Everybody knows Willis Reed. This could be our Willis Reed moment!"

George Michael: I later asked him, "How in the world did you get the strength to go back in there with that knee?" And he said, "You don't think I was going to let Jay Schroeder steal our spotlight."

Doug Williams: When I went back in the game, the guys said, "Let's give him time," because I couldn't move out of my own shadow. They gave me all the time I needed. Players are funny. Players know players. I think that team believed in me more than they believed in Schroeder. He was a little distant. A little arrogant. A little selfish. All the players knew it. Black, white—it didn't matter.

Al Jury, field judge: Doug was always a leader. He once got on one of his Tampa Bay linemen for not dropping a guy: "You've got to cut that man! Cut them damn legs!" I could hear him from way out where I was, chewing him out as he went back to the huddle. That's just the way Doug was. He just didn't believe you could beat him.

Tom Friend: And then the quarter of all quarters begins. It was like a whirlwind, the most amazing thing you ever saw.

Doug Williams: As a player, you don't think of being in the zone. That's more or less for announcers and the media. As a player, you're just trying to carry out the game plan. It was almost like, "Let's get the ball and score again." After the game was over, you think about it and say, Damn, how in the world did we do that?

On his first play after the injury, Williams abandoned the called short pass and instead hit Ricky Sanders with a gorgeous eighty-yard touchdown strike to make the score 10–7. After Denver was forced to punt, Williams—enjoying excellent protection from his offensive line—led the team on a drive that concluded with a twenty-seven-yard touchdown pass to Gary Clark. On Washington's next possession, rookie running back Tim Smith tore off a fifty-eight-yard touchdown run. Before the half, Williams connected with Sanders on a fifty-yard touchdown pass, then hit Clint Didier to make it 35–10 at intermission.

Dale Hamer: When it was 21–10, I made a return trip to the middle of the field and said the same thing: "Don't worry, the Broncos are better than this. We're going to have a football game." But it didn't happen. Doug just kept throwing it up, and they kept scoring.

Doug Williams: At halftime we're up 35–10, and Joe Bugel, the offensive line coach, comes to me. He used to call me Stud. He says, "Hey, Stud, if you don't want to, you ain't got to go back the second half." And I said, "Coach, I started this one, I'm going to finish it."

Tom Friend: The Broncos couldn't handle the Redskins offensive line. Doug had an immense amount of time to throw the football. No one was getting near him. And you know, Doug had one of the game's great arms. I don't think people realize how great his arm was. He had receivers running everywhere.

Kevin Carroll: It was done—done! The Broncos were crushed, and I was screaming and yelling. My boys were screaming and yelling! It was unbelievable—everything that happened. There were so many wonderful turns. The Redskins got some good bounces, and things just worked out for them. It was beautiful. It truly was. You couldn't have scripted a better performance. Doug Williams limped off the field, came back, and orchestrated that amazing game.

George Michael: It was the ultimate warrior game. I think every guy on the team simply said, "We will not let you down." That to me is the ultimate compliment, when the whole team says, "Hey, QB, we'll carry you."

J.C. Watts: For sixty minutes, he did everything a quarterback is supposed to do. If you don't look at his skin color, you'd just say, "Man, the quarterback played well, and the Redskins won." But fact is, he went out and denounced all the myths that corporate America holds about the black man.

Al Conway, umpire: In my twenty-eight years in the league, I never saw a better performance by a quarterback. Montana had some good days. Elway had many good days. Fran Tarkenton and Johnny Unitas too. But the way Williams used Ricky Sanders was great. He and Williams had career days. When you're down like that and you score five times in succession and completely blow the other team out? That takes great leadership.

Dale Hamer: Doug Williams was the best in the world on that day. I don't think any of his fellow quarterbacks would question that. Those touchdowns weren't just dump-offs in the backfield; they were vertical passes. In fact, Johnny Grier, the back judge, was running so hard on a couple of them, he fell down. The grass was a little damp, and he made the Super Bowl XXII highlight film because on two or three of those passes, as he put on the brakes in the end zone, his feet went out from under him. He gave the touchdown signal from a seated position.

George Michael: Each pass was letter-perfect. The line gave him protection. They just said, "We're not gonna let anyone touch you." And after he twisted his knee, they never touched him again. When you look back at the great Super Bowl victories—I was there when Bradshaw threw those touchdowns to Stallworth and Swann—there are certain games where you don't forget the plays. And Doug's throws were one after the other right on the money. He didn't miss. For a while there, he was in a groove that was hard to believe.

The Redskins went on to win Super Bowl XXII 42–10. Williams completed 18 of 29 passes for 340 yards and was named the game's MVP. He set four Super Bowl records that magical night: passing yards in a game (340), passing yards in a quarter (228), touchdown passes (four), and longest completion (80 yards). More important, on the sports world's greatest stage, Doug Williams laid to rest the myth that a black man could not be a championship quarterback.

Tom Friend: After that Super Bowl, Doug was the toast of the town. He was the man. I remember the T-shirts, DOUG WILLIAMS:

TOUCH OF CLASS. After he won, that's what everybody wore. They threw him a Doug Williams Day in Washington, and he couldn't make it because he had already promised to be home in Zachary, Louisiana. I think his daughter made him promise to go to Zachary that day. Some guy's quote to him was, "That's okay, because you don't see Lincoln or Washington showing up for Presidents' Day."

Joe Greene: It was as if I had won the championship, as if I was down there on the field. I was as happy for Doug as I'd be for myself. It was a special moment—a historic moment.

Danny Barrett: For Doug to get off the ground with what appeared to be a career-ending knee injury, then come back and play the way he did, it inspired many young men, especially black quarterbacks, to stick with the position.

Michael Vick, quarterback, Atlanta Falcons: I was seven years old. I'd just started watching football. I was a big Elway fan. I'd never seen a black quarterback before. When I saw Doug Williams beat Denver, I was like, Damn, he's throwing the ball—touchdown passes!—just running the offense. I said to myself, Dude, he's doing his thing. He's really handling his business.

The Rev. Jesse Jackson: When the Redskins returned to Washington, he went straight to the campus of Howard University for a rally. He was making a statement about the connection between Grambling State and Howard. He was sensitive to the social dynamics of that victory.

Randall Cunningham: He'll never know how much it meant to me when he called me up after the Super Bowl. I said, "Hey, man, I'm out here, and I just want to congratulate you and give you a hug." He took the time to say, "Hey, brother, I share this with you."

Mike Adamle, TV commentator, former Kansas City Chiefs running back: I was working the sideline for ABC, and I had a chance to interview him after the game. He was sequestered off in a private training room. Eddie Robinson was there by his side. He was just so overcome with emotion, not just from winning the Super Bowl, but from knowing what it meant in the long term. He was totally spent, totally exhausted. It was like the weight of the world had been lifted off his shoulders.

Doug Williams: Keith Jackson interviewed me on TV, and at the end of the interview, he said, "Thank you, sir." It was like a sign of respect, you know? I think he realized what I'd gone through. He was trying to say, "This man deserves some accolades."

J.C. Watts: Donovan McNabb, Michael Vick, and all the black quarterbacks of today owe a great deal to James Harris and Jefferson Street Joe. They owe a lot to Warren Moon. But I think the person that actually got the black quarterback over the hump was Doug Williams.

Charles Ross: When you look at his performance, you have to say it was the greatest performance by a quarterback in the history of the Super Bowl, because no other quarterback ever had to take on that kind of responsibility and anxiety and perform at that level.

George Michael: From the get-go, the whole city was behind him. There's a guy named Fred Fila who ran a company called Shirt Explosion, and Shirt Explosion would make shirts with various depictions of the Redskins. Well, they came out with a shirt that said JUST CALL ME POCKET. Pocket was Doug's nickname, because he'd always say to the offensive line, "Boys, I ain't going nowhere but right here." That shirt? They couldn't print it fast enough. It just struck a nerve. Didn't matter if you were black, white, yellow—everybody loved Doug Williams. For that year, he hit a high note that not many Redskins had ever seen before.

Eddie Sapir, Doug Williams' former agent: With endorsements, the measuring stick was what Phil Simms got the year before. Doug certainly didn't do better than Simms. Was it because Doug was African-American? I had the guy from L.A. Gear wanting him real bad. In those days, every beautiful lady running around Hollywood, they were all into those little pink-and-white shoes, and L.A. Gear was getting big. They wanted the MVP of the Super Bowl. But they were lowballing him, saying Doug's not exactly a fashion plate. Look at the size of his foot, they said. That's the way a lot of that stuff was. Doug made some money, but it wasn't anything astronomical. He took care of his family, his mom, his dad, who was real sick at the time, his brothers, his sisters. They almost all lived on one street in Zachary, Lemon Road. He took care of everybody.

Tom Friend: The first game of the following season, he had a shoe deal with this company, and the shoe just literally fell apart. I said, "How's the shoe?" after the game. And he said, "It sucked!" He never wore it again.

Eddie Sapir: We made the Disney World deal around two in the morning. I told them, "Why don't we just cut to the chase? What's the deal with Elway?" They said $25,000. And I said, 'Look, I'm tired. I'm sure you all are tired. Everybody knows Elway's going to win it. Why don't you just offer Doug $75,000?'" I was just kinda outshooting them, and we got $75,000.

After two more seasons with the Redskins, Williams retired. He began his coaching career at Louisiana's Northeast High School before moving on to the U.S. Naval Academy, the Scottish Claymores of the World Football League, Morehouse College, and finally, in 1998, Grambling State University, where he succeeded the great Eddie Robinson. From 2000 to 2002, Williams led his alma mater to three consecutive SWAC titles. He currently serves as a personnel executive for the Tampa Bay Buccaneers.

Doug Williams: After the game, I went and hugged Coach Robinson. He was ecstatic, emotional. Told me that was the proudest football moment in his life. He said, "Doug, you might not understand this, but what happened today had the same impact as Joe Louis vs. Max Schmeling. Twenty to thirty years from now, you'll understand."

Charles Ross: Doug Williams' Super Bowl wasn't as big as Joe Louis winning the heavyweight championship or Jackie Robinson breaking the color barrier in baseball, but it was big. African-Americans across the country felt a rush of pride mixed with relief, and also a bit of guarded optimism that this was going to open the floodgates, that other teams were going to jump on the bandwagon. But that didn't happen. You didn't see much of Doug Williams after the Super Bowl. You didn't see him doing TV commercials. You didn't see him signing big endorsement deals, running around on the speaking circuit, or appearing on talk shows. Nothing like what happened—before or since—to winning Super Bowl quarterbacks who happened to be white.

Doug Williams: I run across a lot of people today, and they always say the same thing: "I got that tape. When I'm feeling down, I pop that tape in." Or: "Son, I just want to tell you, I don't know nothing about football, but I want to let you know, I pray for you."

Joe Gilliam at his football camp, 2000.

CHAPTER 8

SCARS

"I want to live the rest of my life in peace. That's why I'm doing this interview. I got money. I got enough to keep me busy. I want to have that peace, too."
—WARREN MOON

Football is a game of sacrifice. It's virtually impossible to take the field without leaving a part of yourself behind—knees, vertebrae, cartilage. For African-American quarterbacks, however, the toll is even greater. How much can you attribute their personal problems to the pain of their struggles? Hard to say. But each has his demons. Joe Gilliam and Eldridge Dickey both suffered from drug addiction and both died young. And, on January 31, 1988, as Doug Williams scaled the sport's summit, proving once and for all that there was no limit to what a black quarterback can do, Marlin Briscoe—twelve years removed from a very fruitful, very successful career as a wide receiver—found himself struggling in prison to preserve his life.

Marlin Briscoe: To be honest with you, I was in jail for drug possession. It was tough because everybody knew who I was. The inmates were looking at me. But Doug [Williams'] performance made me feel better. I think I was living through him. When he led the Redskins back, it was just unbelievable. There were a lot of grown men crying. For the black inmates, it was like he had liberated them. Because, for one reason or another—especially in the black community—sports is a way to escape the realities of daily life. That's why people relate so much to athletes. It gives them a reason to cheer.

Roy S. Johnson: The early pioneers faced obstacles most people in sports could not even fathom. They had broken barriers just by being able to play quarterback, not only through high school, but in college too. But that didn't earn them anything. They still faced a perception—*a belief*—that a black man was not capable of playing the position. A belief that was ingrained in the coaches, executives, and fans, who looked at it as their glory position—the guy you want your daughter to date.

Skip Bayless: In 1976, when I was a young reporter at the *Los Angeles Times*, I was assigned a story on this kid named Doug Williams at Grambling. Before I went to meet him, I thought, "Well, gee, I should call one of the prominent GMs of the day." He immediately told me, off the record, that the team didn't have a lot of use for Doug Williams. He didn't think Doug *thought* well enough to be a professional quarterback. Doug was six-four, 220, with not just a good arm but an all-time big arm—a bazooka arm. If you put those dimensions in the computer without the color attached, it would have spit out first pick in the draft!

James Harris: When I left Los Angeles in '77, the reality hit me— America wasn't ready for a black quarterback. The facts are what they are: There were no other black quarterbacks starting in the NFL. From 1969 to 1977, with the exception of Joe Gilliam and me, nobody else really started. *Nobody in America was good enough to make it in the NFL as a black quarterback?*

Roy S. Johnson: This was long before we had African-Americans in positions of significant leadership in government. It was long before we had African-Americans in positions of leadership in business. [When Williams and Harris were born,] we were still living in Jim Crow times, times when segregation ruled, and, while there were positions of leadership in the African-American community, those rarely translated outside the community. So it wasn't surprising that the NFL, one of the most visible and popular bastions in sports, reflected that same reluctance.

There clearly were instances where white teammates did not want to take orders from black quarterbacks, instances where they didn't want to listen to someone of color because, in many cases, they had never even associated with people of color. To be subservient to an African-American was probably their worst nightmare. But, at the end of the day, most of them came around. It was the coaches and executives who showed the most resistance.

The Rev. Jesse Jackson: Could a black play center? Could a black play middle linebacker? Could a black play quarterback? Could a black coach? Every step has been like a major political battle. It's the nature of the politics of our culture that always limits the opportunity.

Roy S. Johnson: Many quarterbacks undermined their own performances by running slower in the forty, by maybe dropping balls on passing drills to try to prevent coaches and executives from thinking, Well, maybe I can play this guy at another position. While it was smart, it was also sad. It was sad that anyone with talent, that anyone with skills, that anyone who had leadership capability and the ability to excel was forced to diminish himself just to get the opportunity to do what he loves.

Harry Edwards: Blacks have always had the capability to be quarterbacks, but they were not given the opportunity, largely because of racism. They were not believed to have the intellectual capacity to play the position. What changed was not brotherhood, but business—the dynamics and realities of the game. When you have people coming off the end like Jevon Kearse, Charles Haley, and Derrick Thomas, it's bad business to have a wooden, pocket-passing kind of guy back there. Why? Because he's going to get concussions. He's gonna get beat up.

What gave us the black quarterback was good football business. What gave us the black quarterback was Derrick Thomas and Charles Haley and Reggie White, just as surely as the lion gave the antelope his speed. This is something that colleges and universities found out in the 1980s.

If it had to do with brotherhood, we'd have more than six black coaches at the Division I-A level in college. We would have more black coaches in the NFL.

Jimmy Raye: The number of players with ability has changed, but the other thing driving the rise in opportunity is the football environment: As a coach, you have a two- or three-year window in which to be successful. You can't afford to be indifferent to a guy who can help you win—and quickly.

Ken Riley: It's all about the fans, the people sitting in the stands. In my time, I don't think the public was ready for it, even the situation with Joe Gilliam in Pittsburgh. I think Coach Noll liked Gilliam. He played him. But you've got to fill those stands.

Roy S. Johnson: It's hard to articulate how painful it is to know that you're as good if not better than everyone else—to know that you're capable of succeeding and yet have that taken away because of something that has nothing to do with anything but the color of your skin. The pain of that, the impact of that, ate away at these early quarterbacks, just as it ate away at African-Americans in other segments of society. That is why many of them went on to have difficult lives. Because the pain and the burden of racism does not go away when the final buzzer sounds; it doesn't go away when you take off the uniform.

Judge Dickson: You become very distrustful. In a discriminatory environment, you're constantly thinking, Am I being treated unfairly, or is this happening because of my color? It can be a huge inhibitor, a terrible burden for a young person to have. And if you talk about it, you're a complainer, a whiner. It's a downward spiral.

Brigman Owens: In Dallas, there were places where we couldn't eat, places where we couldn't live as black athletes. The black players had to eat at the Howard Johnson. Smorgasbord on Thursday, fish on Friday, and Italian on Saturday. I remember that to this day.

They wanted the black athletes to live in South Dallas, which was a very bad area, whereas the white players lived in very nice apartments. I was a Dallas Cowboy! We were supposed to be ambassadors for the city! I remember complaining that I couldn't find a place to live. They told me I wasn't in California or Ohio. The attitude toward me changed. They always say I missed one tackle against the Vikings, but the bigger reason for my fall from grace was that I had complained about the conditions. That's why I said *thank God* when I was traded to Washington.

Charles Garcia: Choo Choo Brackins once tried out with the Dallas Texans. Before practice, he was throwing the ball, just throwing it around, and Hank Stram told him, "Put that ball down. You're playing with the defensive backs." Choo didn't want any controversy, but that just broke his heart.

Judge Dickson: Sandy Stephens never really got the desire to play quarterback in the NFL out of his system. Looking back on his football career, you realize he had these huge accomplishments. But some stuff tore at him. He wanted to be a success as a pro, and he did not attain that. It left a very bad taste in his mouth. This was a tremendous competitor. To go on after that was a tough adjustment.

Warren Moon: A lot of this stuff, you keep inside you. You can't really talk about it. Who's going to understand? Unless you played quarterback, you don't know quarterback. And when you're a black quarterback, you can't talk to anybody. So you tend to keep it inside. When you do interviews, you try to give everything a positive spin. You don't want to bring out the garbage because it sounds like you're whining.

I'm in therapy right now. I have a lot of anger, a lot of frustration. My therapist feels I hid a lot of stuff away and didn't deal with it. I tried to keep everything under control, tried to handle things as if everything was all right. At a young age you can do that, but as you get older you just don't have the patience.

Marlin Briscoe: I think about what if? If I was a flop then it wouldn't have been as significant. If I stunk, I shouldn't have been playing. But the fact that I still hold records in Denver after all these years and yet I wasn't able to compete…what kind of justice is that?

Vince Evans: We were expected to be almost supernatural. Because we had these athletic talents, these strong arms, we were expected to make throws that other quarterbacks could not throw, to win games others could not.

The white quarterback? Man, he could make a ton of mistakes and he would never get berated, never get put down in a meeting. But me? "Vince, didn't you see that? It's obvious to all of us here that you shouldn't have thrown that pass."

Judge Dickson: To the day he died, Sandy Stephens resented the fact that, while he was in high school, he wasn't selected to the first string of Fayette, Pennsylvania's all-county team—so much so that he vowed he would not be buried in Fayette. That's how much it hurt him.

James Harris: You have to remember another thing about those years: The other three guys in my position got involved in drugs. What if I had been the fourth? We wouldn't have had nobody. If I hadn't played during that time, how different would it have been for the guys after me?

Marlin Briscoe: I look at myself, Eldridge Dickey, Joe Gilliam, and James Harris—three out of four of us had drug problems. Shack's mindset was different. Joe, Eldridge, and myself probably lived on the edge a little more, partying with girls and all that stuff. We were more vulnerable. Even though I was successful, won two rings, got out of the game unhurt, in a great financial position, I often think that the pain and disappointment of not being able to continue my career as a quarterback might have seeped into my psyche. I'm not speaking for Joe and Eldridge, but the three of us were prone to drug issues. Two of them died, and I sit here. God spared me.

Roy S. Johnson: When James Harris, when Marlin Briscoe and Joe Gilliam took the snap from center, it was like all of Black America was taking that snap. When they completed a pass, it was as if all of Black America was completing that pass. When they fumbled, it was if all African-Americans were fumbling that ball. They carried that burden with them, just as many other pioneers did. It was a heavy burden, one that certainly affected their ability to succeed, to deal with the ups and downs that invariably come with playing such a high-profile position in professional sports.

Vince Evans: You are constantly under pressure, under stress, not only to lead the team, but also to prove—even to the *brothers*—that you can get it done. That leash is tight on your neck. You just don't have the leeway to make mistakes.

Warren Moon: Football was a comfort zone for me. My family was a comfort zone. When I retired, not only did my career end, so did my marriage. My whole support structure was gone. I've been living in an abyss for the last five years, trying to figure out where I'm going. I'm busy, but I don't have the same direction. When I played football, I knew my goals. Now it's totally different.

Stoicism assumes a different meaning for African-American quarterbacks. In addition to playing when hurt, ignoring injuries, and picking yourself up off the ground after being leveled, you're expected to endure the intellectual and emotional slings. Those who do not or cannot—like Joe Gilliam and Eldridge Dickey—look forward to short, frustrating careers.

Marlin Briscoe: Drug addiction cost me everything. My family: I had a baby girl—we're just now starting to mend fences. It cost me my house. I had a vineyard and an acre-and-a-half of property. I had a good job—selling municipal bonds and government securities—and a car. All those things went out the window one by one. I didn't care. You don't care as long as the drugs are there. It got worse and worse and worse. I was homeless. I went from doing drugs in my house to the streets. You lose your dignity. The one thing that helped me is the fact that I still worked out. Even when I'd go days on a binge of drug use, I always found time to work out, play basketball, run. I guess I was a functional junkie.

Floyd Little: I saw Marlin once during that time, and I didn't recognize him. The man I knew was a great athlete, and now he was down to 140 pounds. He was a year or two out of the league. What would you think? He came out to Denver seeking some help, which I don't think he got. He played in Denver only for a year. But he was my teammate. Once a teammate, always a teammate. I don't care if it's for a day.

He looked horrible. Horrible. He had changed a couple of shades in color, his lips were ashen, he was twitchy, and it seemed as though he was nervous. He wasn't the Marlin Briscoe I knew. He was always a strong, prideful man, but he didn't have that confidence anymore. You looked at him and you knew he had a problem.

Warren Moon: Talking like this—sitting down with another man and talking about some of these things—I'd never do that when I was in my thirties. I was invincible. But one of the things that helped was listening to James, listening to Doug, and listening to Vince tell their stories. I didn't play when James played. I didn't play when Marlin played. I played with Vince, but we weren't close. We were competitors. I didn't want to expose any weaknesses.

Vince Evans: I knew about the James Harrises, the Doug Williamses, the Joe Gilliams. But there were many more I didn't know. Once you understand what those guys went through, you pull back a layer and look at the Willie Throwers and USC's Willie Woods, guys like that. Because I didn't have the opportunity to talk to those guys, it felt like no one else knew exactly what I was dealing with. I got so caught up in fighting my own battles that I didn't realize how many guys were in the fight with me—not until it was over.

Warren Moon: From the very beginning, we saw what the unlevel playing field did to Joe Gilliam. Joe suffered from drug abuse and a lot of it had to do with the bitterness, the unfairness with which he was treated in Pittsburgh. He never got over that.

In the end, it wasn't curfew infractions, missed meetings, or poor play-calling, but cocaine that derailed Joe Gilliam's career. He simply could not conquer his addiction. With the help of his father, he eventually pulled himself together and started a football camp for children at Tennessee State, which included drug counseling. But it seems that Gilliam never completely recovered from the psychological trauma of his time in the NFL.

Brad Pye Jr.: Joe wasn't strong enough mentally. He wasn't strong enough to overcome racism. He just thought things should be fair and the world isn't fair.

Ernie Holmes: Joey went through an onslaught of changes: He got so addicted to cocaine, he started using crack cocaine. His father got him into a rehab program and he done good for awhile, but when he got out, he got back into drugs.

Just before he died, we had a twenty-fifth anniversary celebration for our Super Bowl IX win and we had a fabulous time. Joe was telling me about how his life had changed, how he was working with the Boy Scouts and the Lord was blessing him. He said they were doing a movie about his life. But I think he started doing cocaine again. Soon after that, he had a massive heart attack. He had been staying at the YMCA in Tennessee. He was down on his luck.

Rocky Bleier: For all the bravado we saw on the outside, inside Joe there was a whole lot of insecurity. He wasn't a big guy. There was some question about whether he could take the beating. I think part of his escapism, his depression, the rejection he felt, was offset by drugs. When he was taking drugs, I'm sure he felt better, more confident in his ability. I'm not saying he got into drugs because he got benched. It was a combination of factors.

Doug Williams: I wasn't going to miss the funeral. I thought I owed it to Joe and to myself. It was snowing that day. I'll never forget it. To me, Joe's death was a great loss. When I think of Joe, I put him in the same category as James Harris. To me, James Harris epitomizes what I always wanted to be. He, Joe, and my oldest brother are probably my biggest inspirations.

In 1971, my junior year in high school, Joe Gilliam was playing quarterback at Tennessee State and he came to play Southern University in Baton Rouge. When he walked out of the dressing room, I was standing right by the fence. I saw this skinny little bean. I said, "Shoot, if he can play, I can play."

Marlin Briscoe: Joe Gilliam's father wanted to do something to honor Joe on his birthday. He wanted to bring together all the black quarterbacks who had played in the NFL. This was in 2002, right after Michael Vick's rookie year. So he extended invitations to all of us to come to Nashville for this huge banquet. A couple thousand people showed up, kids and their parents, to get autographs. The response was overwhelming.

They marched us down to the stage by year—from the most recent quarterback to the first. I was the last one introduced. I got a standing ovation.

James and Doug were doing something for the Black College All-Stars, so they weren't there. They spoke by video. But the turnout was amazing: Michael Vick, Kordell Stewart, Donovan McNabb, Steve McNair, Joe Hamilton, Aaron Brooks, Vince Evans, Warren Moon, Jarius Jackson, Daunte Culpepper, Randall Cunningham, Shaun King.

Joe Gilliam Sr.: Progress comes with a price. Somebody's got to pay. Joe paid with his life. That's why all those guys came to his memorial—the greatest assembly of black quarterbacks in the history of the NFL.

Warren Moon: We had a little private meeting beforehand, about eight or nine of us in a room. Everybody started telling stories. That's when we said, "Hey this is something we need to keep going, we need to keep all of us together, form some type of fraternity to let the young guys know who we are."

Doug Williams: About a week later, one of the strangest things happened. James and I were in Atlanta. Neither one of us had planned this, mind you. We ran up on each other in the airport. And it wasn't ten minutes later that Warren Moon came up the escalator. It was almost like an omen. We got to talking and exchanged numbers, and before long, the Field Generals were born—in the food court in the airport in Atlanta.

Warren Moon: I was just getting off a redeye. It was, like, six in the morning. And we ended up going to Popeye's Chicken for breakfast. Popeye's Chicken in Concourse B.

Marlin Briscoe: I wasn't part of the initial conversation. Shack called me and told me what they were proposing. I said, "Man, that's an excellent idea." So we got the ball rolling. That's how we founded the Field Generals.

The Field Generals is a non-profit organization dedicated to teaching and preserving the history of the African-American quarterback.

Warren Moon: One of the things I regret is that I didn't become closer friends with Doug and the others when I was playing. We could have helped each other through the tough times. That's one reason we started this group, so guys could have a dialogue. If we had done that while we were playing, it might have lifted some of the burden.

Vince Evans: What's interesting is that I don't think the Field Generals would have come together had Joe Gilliam not died.

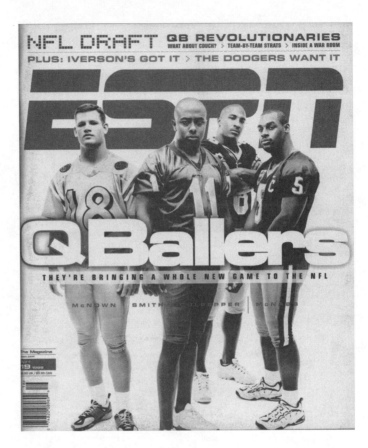

Quarterbacks (from left) Cade McNown, Akili Smith, Daunte Culpepper, and Donovan McNabb on the cover of *ESPN The Magazine*, April 19, 1999.

CHAPTER NINE

FORWARD PROGRESS

*"We've shown we can lead. We've shown we can win. But is it accepted?
Not by everybody. No matter how much success we have, there's always
going to be a handful of people who can't stand what we're doing."*
—DONOVAN MCNABB, PHILADELPHIA EAGLES

Despite the advances of African-American quarterbacks in the 1980s—from Warren Moon's lucrative contract with the Houston Oilers to Doug Williams' momentous Super Bowl performance—pro football continued to exhibit reservations about black college quarterbacks; throughout the decade, not a single one was chosen in the first round of the NFL draft. When the Philadelphia Eagles picked UNLV's Randall Cunningham in the second round in 1985, he was viewed largely as a backup to veteran Ron Jaworski. However, Cunningham's innovative and dynamic playmaking soon caught the attention of the Eagles coaching staff. Within two seasons, he would become Philadelphia's starter and a highlight-reel staple. Avoiding the pass rush, launching deep throws *with accuracy, and breaking out on his own for first-down yardage, Cunningham was the Eagles' leading rusher in each year from 1987 to 1990.*

Jimmie Giles: Guys like Randall Cunningham really changed perceptions. If you don't have an offensive line to protect you, you've got to get out and do what's best for the team—make plays.

Lovie Smith: Randall Cunningham made you play things more honestly. James Harris was a dropback quarterback. Doug Williams was not a big running quarterback; he stayed in the pocket most of the time. But Cunningham—he was able to do what the Mike Vicks of today do.

Michael Vick: He had everyone in the neighborhood dropping back saying, "Randall Cunningham! Randall Cunningham!"

Jimmie Giles: When we played together in Tampa, Doug Williams and I perfected the post pattern. Growing up, Randall loved that play, but he didn't know how to throw it, didn't have people who could run it, so we worked on it together all the time.

One Monday night against the Giants, we were supposed to run that play. I'm going to my left, trying to get open, when I saw Carl Banks hit Randall in the backfield. Randall jumps up and somehow gets the throw off for a touchdown. It was the most unbelievable play I've ever seen a quarterback make.

Little by little, NFL teams began to view black quarterbacks as franchise players. In 1990, the University of Houston's Andre Ware, the first African-American quarterback to win the Heisman Trophy, became the first black quarterback in twenty-one years to be chosen in the first round of the draft. Five years later, the Houston Oilers drafted Alcorn State's Steve McNair with the third overall pick. In the end, Ware started only six games for the Detroit Lions, leaving for the CFL after a series of injuries and a lack of playing time. But McNair transformed what would become the Tennessee Titans into a perennial contender. An excellent pocket passer with an unusual ability to absorb hits and shed defenders, he added a new dimension to the team's offense with his explosive running skills. In 2000, he became the second African-American quarterback to take a team to the Super Bowl. The Titans lost to the Rams 23–16 on the game's final play when Tennessee receiver Kevin Dyson was tackled one yard shy of the tying touchdown.

But it was the milestone celebrated the previous spring that said the most about where things were headed. On April 17, 1999, Syracuse's Donovan McNabb, Central Florida's Daunte Culpepper, and Oregon's Akili Smith all became first-round draft picks. For the first time in history, three of the first eleven players chosen were black quarterbacks.

Tony Dungy: That draft was when I thought, We've made it, we've progressed. You had six or seven guys who inspired a lot of back-and-forth on the radio talk shows. "Hey, do you like Tim Couch? Donovan McNabb? Akili Smith? Sean King? Daunte Culpepper? Cade McNown?" Some liked this guy, some liked that guy. I happened to like Akili Smith, and Andy Reid liked McNabb. Everybody had their personal opinion, but it was never about white quarterbacks and black quarterbacks. To me, that was a turning point. It symbolized how far we had come.

Roy S. Johnson: I was in the draft room that day. The fact that McNabb, Smith, and Culpepper were there too was a subtle turning point, because they were being recognized as players who deserved the opportunity to be picked in the first round. The fact that they were selected in the first round was a major turning point. They were allowed to go on the stage and shake the hand of the commissioner as the new faces of their franchises. Two of the three succeeded, one did not. But the fact that Akili Smith's lack of success was not held against other African-American quarterbacks is significant because back in the day, if one of us fell, we all fell.

Glenn Harris, sports anchor, Washington, D.C.: Akili Smith played for a lousy team in the pros. He was a great college quarterback, got a shot at the NFL, and it just didn't work out. But he got paid. He got an opportunity to compete. That's the main thing.

Smith started only seventeen games for the Cincinnati Bengals. He was cut three times, once each by the Bengals, Packers, and Buccaneers, and left the league in 2005. Culpepper won the starting job in his second season in Minnesota, guiding the Vikings to an 11–5 record and the NFC championship game. Three years later, he led the league with 4,717 passing yards, setting a franchise record along the way with thirty-nine touchdown passes. But it was McNabb who emerged as the pride of the class. He piloted the Eagles to four straight NFC championship games and a Super Bowl. He could pass, he could run, and he could lead a team—talents that would mark him as one of the league's top quarterbacks.

Still, despite five trips to the Pro Bowl, he was the object of intense debate. In September 2003, outspoken conservative Rush Limbaugh declared on ESPN's Sunday Countdown that McNabb was overrated by the press simply because he was black. "The media has been very desirous that a black quarterback do well," Limbaugh offered. "There is a little hope invested in McNabb, and he got a lot of credit for the performance of this team that he didn't deserve." Three days later, amid a storm of controversy, Limbaugh resigned from the show.

J.C. Watts: Limbaugh's diatribe crystallized the challenge of the black quarterback. It was baffling. Why Donovan? I mean, his statistics, his performance, his leadership just did not merit those comments.

Wilburn Hollis: Jiminy Christmas, what do you have to do to prove yourself? I'm thinking we're past this, and here comes this jerko. Suddenly, we're back in the dark ages. It pissed me off.

Chuck Ealey: He could've said McNabb was overrated and left it at that. There have been many overrated white quarterbacks in the NFL—too many to name—and nobody ever made an issue of that. McNabb's ability has nothing to do with the color of his skin.

Stephen A. Smith: To me, Rush Limbaugh wasn't talking about Donovan McNabb as much as he was talking about the media. He was wrong. What's to say they root for Donovan McNabb more than they root for Tom Brady? There's no evidence of that. He came across as very ignorant.

But once he was faced with factual information that knocked down his argument, he was defiant in his refusal to address people's concerns about the issue. That's what I couldn't support. Because now it looked like he was just stirring up trouble. To a guy like McNabb, it brought the wrong kind of attention. Instead of McNabb the quarterback, it was his blackness that hit center stage. And Donovan McNabb did not deserve that.

Michael Smith: I think the world of Peyton Manning. He's a phenomenal quarterback, one of the game's all-time greats. But Peyton has been to, what, one conference championship game? It's dogged him, totally dogged him, that he's never been to the Super Bowl, much less won one. But Donovan McNabb has been to four conference championship games and one Super Bowl, which his team lost by *three* points. And yet, he is not perceived to be the kind of quarterback that Peyton is. Why is that?

J.C. Watts: I'm not making excuses for Donovan, but Troy Aikman struggled at some point during his career. Dan Marino struggled. Both those guys are Hall of Famers. Jim Kelly will go down in history as a great quarterback, but he made the Super Bowl four times and never won.

Danny Barrett: Donovan McNabb's numbers speak for themselves. The guy has been to five Pro Bowls. Forget the negativity. McNabb has earned the right to be considered among the best in the league.

The hostility toward McNabb was not limited to one incident nor confined to right-wing commentators. In 2005, near the end of a season marred by injury and a team meltdown fueled by clashes with high-priced free agent Terrell Owens, the quarterback found himself under siege from the president of the Philadelphia chapter of the NAACP. In a scathing newspaper column published in the Philadelphia

Sun, J. Whyatt Mondesire deemed McNabb "mediocre at best," a weak, selfish leader who "played the race card."

Stephen A. Smith: He was basically calling Donovan McNabb a sell-out. That's as inexcusable as it gets. He had no right as a black man to publicly condemn McNabb the way he did. Just because McNabb says, "You know what? I don't want to be known as a scrambling quarterback, don't want to fall into the stereotype of a black quarterback," that gave Mondesire no right to say what he said. Because it made news, it brought attention to an issue that I'm quite sure Donovan McNabb would have preferred to avoid.

Al Jury: McNabb hasn't won the big one yet. Until he does that, he's going to get criticism. If he wins the Super Bowl and gets that monkey off his back, the fans are going to adore him. But when you don't win, they start thinking, What have you done for me lately? I don't think that has anything to do with being a black quarterback.

With each step forward, African-American quarterbacks seemed to invite greater scrutiny. After five NFL seasons in Atlanta, Michael Vick, who was selected with the very first pick in the 2001 draft after leading Virginia Tech to the NCAA national championship game as a freshman, ranked sixth in winning percentage among active quarterbacks. Critics point instead to his fifty-four-percent completion rate and 75.8 QB rating.

Doug Williams: Michael Vick went to the NFC championship game in 2004, and people still scrutinize this kid. They spend so much time trying to find out what the African-American quarterback can't do instead of what he can do. People don't give him the benefit of the doubt. I got into an argument with a guy who said, "Michael Vick ain't no quarterback." I asked him why. He said, "Because he runs around too much." I said, "Quarterback gets up under the center, don't he? Michael Vick is a quarterback."

Danny Barrett: With Michael, people talk about his trouble throwing the football. But at the end of the day, all that matters is whether there's a W on the board. Was the guy efficient, and did he make plays when he had to? That's what Mike does.

Charles Ross: ESPN had me on when Michael Vick was drafted No. 1, and we dealt with the same old question: "Vick's a runner, which means he's an athletic guy, which means…is he smart enough to play quarterback?" None of it open and direct, mind you, but implicit. Now, you don't have those implicit questions when the quarterback in question is white. Fran Tarkenton ran all over the field. Smart? You bet. But nobody asked. Archie Manning wasn't the greatest quarterback when it came to throwing the ball; he was more of a runner. But nobody ever raised any questions about his mental ability.

Gene Upshaw: They still want Vick to be a goddamn pocket passer, but he is what he is. He can beat you with his feet or his arm. Don't try to make him Johnny Unitas.

Michael Vick: I can go into a game, sit in the pocket, do everything I'm supposed to do, complete seventy percent of my passes. I'm accurate, everything is straight drop-back—five-step, seven-step—and they praise me. I come back the next week and do the same thing, but we lose. Then they say I'm not accurate, I can't throw from the pocket.

As good as Donovan McNabb is in the pocket, he still doesn't get the credit he deserves. That's what made me say the hell with it. I'm not trying to please nobody else. I just got to do what I can do, control what I can control.

Donovan McNabb: I personally don't feel that we've turned the corner. People may recognize the success of the black quarterback, but do they accept it? They're always trying to find the deeper reasons for why we succeed—is it because we're good at what we do or because the people around us are good at what they do?

Stephen A. Smith: When you're in a unique position, you have a responsibility to carry yourself and conduct yourself accordingly, to accept the responsibility that goes along with it. It's not just about performance; it's about recognizing the attention that comes because of the position. It may not be fair for the McNabbs, the McNairs, and the Culpeppers, who are being judged by their hue and their ethnicity just as much as by their performance, but it's the reality of the situation. I don't think there's any way around that.

In 2006, after leading Texas to a stunning national-title victory over defending champion USC, Vince Young was poised for stardom. In three years with the Longhorns, he had completed sixty-two percent of his passes for 6,040 yards, all culminating with that MVP performance in the Rose Bowl, where he completed 30 of 40 passes for 267 yards and rushed nineteen times for 200 yards and three touchdowns, including a game-winning eight-yard sprint with nineteen seconds left on the clock. Two months later, he declared himself eligible for the draft. Almost immediately, the questions surfaced: Was his arm strong enough? Did he have the necessary throwing skills? Was he smart enough?

Jimmy Raye: If you asked any general manager in the NFL two hours after that game who the two best players in the country were, Young would have been in that top two. But then the scrutiny started. Everybody was trying to find the flaws.

Jerry Rice: What does a Wonderlic score have to do with anything? I'm sure we've had some white quarterbacks who didn't do well on that test.

Joe Greene: A quarterback has to be able to read defenses. Everybody in college is trying to run complex spread offenses, and nobody did it better than this kid. So why is his test score an issue?

Danny Barrett: It was disappointing to see that happen, especially in the manner in which it was presented. They were trying to take something away from the young man before giving him a chance. It was unfair, to be honest. To see one of the top guys in the history of the college ranks get scrutinized that way, it just goes to show you that there are still unresolved issues.

Gene Upshaw: They were trying to negotiate—to get him as cheap as they could. That's what that shit was about: "We're not sure how smart you are. We're not sure you can read defenses. We're not sure you can play." It's a business, and teams are in negotiation mode.

Randall Cunningham: I grew up a USC fan, and I'm still a USC fan. I was sure there was no way Texas was going to beat the Trojans, but when I saw Vince Young during a timeout on the sideline, it freaked me out. I could see his countenance—total boldness and confidence. And I was like, Wow.

Donovan McNabb: The man had over 400 yards of total offense, and they still don't give him the credit he deserves. When he decided to go pro, they didn't talk about the good things he could do. It was always, "He's not going to be able to get under the center and take a snap." They talked about his throwing motion, saying he's not a passing quarterback. It's like we always have to be *running* quarterbacks or *athletic* quarterbacks.

Jerry Rice: For him to have the composure to run the ball into the end zone on fourth down in the Rose Bowl? That shows everything right there—his intelligence, his decision-making skills, his athletic ability. He's six-feet-five, 230 pounds, he can run like crazy, and he can throw the football with accuracy. He's the real thing.

J.C. Watts: Can I prove that people picked on Vince Young's throwing motion because of his skin color? No. But the thought did cross my mind. I wouldn't give a plugged nickel for Bernie Kosar's throwing motion. From the time he got under center with that half-cocked stand, which goes against everything you're taught, to how slowly he dropped back, to how he threw the ball...Bernie was about as ugly as it got. But you know what? I liked watching Bernie play, because the guy won. His passes may not have been as pretty as Warren Moon's or Dan Marino's, but somehow, he got it there. You can't argue with the guy's record.

The number three pick in the draft, Young opened the 2006 season in Tennessee as a backup to Kerry Collins. He was handed the starting job after the team struggled to an 0–3 record. With Young, the Titans were a more explosive team. In late November, he led them back from a 21–0 fourth-quarter deficit to beat the New York Giants 24–21. And just like that, he had proven that the skills he displayed in the spread offense at Texas translated to the pros.

Like Cunningham, McNabb, and Vick, Young does not fit the classic pocket passer mold. But with each snap, he pushes the game forward just a bit—and however reluctantly, the NFL is following.

Glenn Harris: You definitely have to have a different game plan for guys like that. Most defensive coaches would prefer to go against a quarterback who just stays in the pocket.

Seneca Wallace, quarterback, Seattle Seahawks: People are always going to say we want the stereotypical quarterback. We want him to be six-four, six-five, stay in the pocket, and throw the ball. But the game is evolving. It's not like it was in 1980, when a quarterback didn't have to deal with all of the blitz packages. Now you need a quarterback who can move around and do different things. In the West Coast offense, everything is quick. Bam! Bam! Bam! Throw the ball.

Tony Dungy: We're obviously in a much different era. Donovan McNabb has been in the Super Bowl. Black quarterbacks have been

Pro Bowlers. Warren Moon was just inducted into the Hall of Fame. Because of those kinds of successes, I think we're very, very close to this being a nonissue.

Seneca Wallace: I don't feel like I've got to prove myself to anybody. I've been in the league three years now. My coaching staff knows what I'm capable of doing, knows I can play. As long as you can throw the ball, throw it consistently, and make all the right reads, there's nothing else to prove.

Ron Meeks: I don't think you have the old stereotypes anymore. Black quarterbacks are given the same opportunities as everybody else.

Daunte Culpepper, quarterback, Miami Dolphins: In my eyes, I see everybody as a quarterback. In this day and age, it shouldn't matter if you're black or white. If you work hard, do everything it takes to be successful, the door should be open. There shouldn't be any barriers.

The Jacksonville Jaguars' three quarterbacks (from left): Byron Leftwich; David Garrard; and Quinn Gray, 2005.

EPILOGUE

The only thing I did was wrong
Was stayin' in the wilderness too long
Keep your eyes on the prize, Hold on
Only thing we did was right
Was the day we started to fight!
Keep your eyes on the prize, Hold on
—ALICE WINE

If it seems that the early Field Generals struggled in vain, consider this: *Joe Gilliam died of a heart attack four days before his fiftieth birthday, on Christmas Day 2000, while watching a Monday Night Football game between the Tennessee Titans and the Dallas Cowboys—a showdown that featured two starting black quarterbacks, Anthony Wright and Steve McNair. Six years later, Warren Moon was inducted into the Hall of Fame. At the time, there were seven African-American quarterbacks starting for NFL teams and twenty overall on league rosters. Three of them—Byron Leftwich, David Garrard, and Quinn Gray—play in Jacksonville, where James "Shack" Harris is the vice president of player personnel. Not only have the numbers changed, but so have the possibilities.*

Warren Moon: You talk about power? These guys have a lot more than we did. When I was in the league, there were five other African-American quarterbacks at most. There was always the possibility you could be tossed out. In some ways, I wanted to speak up. In other ways, I wanted to hide. As soon as someone came up and asked, "When did you stop being a black quarterback?" I was like, "Man, I don't want to deal with that right now. Everything's going well. I don't want to talk about it." But if Michael Vick wanted to say anything on the subject, he could. Same with Donovan McNabb.

The Rev. Jesse Jackson: Today, when Alabama plays Mississippi, you have players on both sides, black and white, and you're pulling for uniform color, not skin color. Here's a white guy hoping that a black guy knocks down another white guy or that a black guy helps a white guy knock a black guy down. Only that field of play allows for the kind of objectivity that takes us to the next level. In so many ways, the political order has not led us there. The church has not led us there. The athletic arena has been the signal for social advancement.

Vince Evans: There's always going to be controversy. But there are enough positive examples to fortify young quarterbacks in the belief that they can play the position. If they're willing to work hard, dedicate themselves, they can not be denied.

Michael Smith: I grew up believing that playing quarterback in the NFL was something I could do. When Steve McNair entered the league as the third pick in 1995, I was sixteen years old. Six years later, Michael Vick went No. 1. That's just something I'm accustomed to: Vick being a superstar, Vince Young being the next best thing, Donovan McNabb leading a team to the Super Bowl. Back when Kordell Stewart was a rookie and the Steelers turned him into Slash, I didn't look at the social ramifications. I thought, Hey, this dude is a double threat. When I saw Warren Moon doing his thing, I wasn't aware of the path he'd taken. All I knew was, here's this guy wearing No.1, putting up 527 yards in a single game against the Chiefs. I didn't know he was breaking stereotypes. I just thought he was breaking records.

Nelson George, novelist and cultural critic: When Doug Williams got to the Super Bowl, it was the crystallization of years of hope. It proved black people could be decision makers. Black people could lead a team to the pinnacle of the sport, which means that black people could be leaders in America at its highest pinnacles. For a black person to be at the center of all the action, the entire stadium waiting for him to make his move, that's an amazing position of power.

Michael Smith: The new challenge is crossover—moving beyond the African-American community. When a guy like Donovan McNabb starts crossing over, becoming a pitchman—not just for Nike, but for Campbell's Soup—he enters a land once reserved for white quarterbacks. When he starts making $100 million, he's viewed as a company man, buddy-buddy with the owner.

Having talked to Donovan, I understand where this leads: He doesn't just have to battle his white critics; he has to battle his African-American critics, too. It's like moving up to the house on the hill. Once you get the big contract—become the face of the organization—it's a little tougher to relate to the guy on the bottom.

Roy S. Johnson: In the future, Donovan McNabb might thank Rush Limbaugh for putting the spotlight on him because he has certainly responded. He has guided his team to the Super Bowl and he is recognized as one of the top quarterbacks in the NFL. He may not tell you this, he may not acknowledge it, but part of his motivation has to be to dispel the Rush Limbaughs of the world. When he looks back on his career, he'll have to look at that moment as a turning point because it gave him extra motivation and Donovan responded. He's played well and, thanks to Limbaugh, a lot of Americans know who Donovan McNabb is.

Michael MacCambridge: The success of players like McNabb, Vick, and Young has had an impact on the conventional wisdom in pro football. To see Vince Young, looking sharp and composed, lead his team to victory from twenty-one points down the way he did against the Giants his rookie year is to see the value of a quarterback with a wide range of skills. It forces you to redefine the ideal quarterback. So things are changing, and they're changing because people like McNabb and Vick and Young *made* them change.

Donovan NcNabb: Byron Leftwich called me last night. We talk all the time. We push for each other and we want to see success. We want to get to the point were there are two African Americans in the Super Bowl. We talk about that all the time.

Some might point to those statements as proof that the African-American quarterback has arrived, proof that the NFL is colorblind. I tend to believe the league has simply embraced the inescapable reality of a new wide-open style of play.

In the last three decades, white skill position players have grown increasingly rare. African-Americans make up virtually all of the NFL's running backs, wide receivers, defensive linemen, cornerbacks, safeties, punt returners, and kick returners. The tight end, fullback, and linebacker positions are being steadily Africanized as well. Is quarterback the next position to go? "It all depends on how much the game evolves," says Byron Leftwich. "If you can still win by throwing the ball in the pocket, no. But if the man behind center has got to be able to run to win, then I think you'll see that change." Thanks to Marlin Briscoe, Randall Cunningham, Donovan McNabb, Michael Vick, and Vince Young, you can't dismiss the value of mobility. It's a critical part of any quarterback's job—right up there with arm strength, accuracy, poise and leadership. Nonetheless I sense a clear longing to move beyond the black quarterback designation. In his Hall of Fame induction speech, Warren Moon—now a radio analyst for the Seahawks and executive vice president of Leigh Steinberg Enterprises—remarked, "A lot has been said about me being the first African-American quarterback to make the Hall of Fame. It's a subject that I'm very uncomfortable about sometimes, because I've always wanted to be judged as just a quarterback." How far is Moon's wish from reality? It all depends on your perspective.

Marlin Briscoe: Warren was so successful, he was the first to break the "black quarterback" moniker. You don't think of Michael Vick and those guys in terms of color. When they play well, they get lauded. When they play badly, they get criticized—just as it should be.

Aaron Brooks, quarterback, Oakland Raiders: The issue isn't dead. To white America, the position is too important to say it's dead. It'll never be dead. As long as we play the position, they'll have something to talk about.

Tony Dungy: We've come to the point where the general public is saying, "Hey, I like Donovan McNabb" or "I like Michael Vick." Those guys have been accepted as the legitimate best at their position.

Looking back, Doug Williams' Super Bowl win has become a landmark in the African-American athlete's hard road to glory, but there are many smaller victories. Much like James Harris, who worked his way up the front office ladder, Williams has moved from high school coach in Louisiana, to running backs coach at Navy, to offensive coordinator with the Scottish Claymores, to head coach at Morehouse College and Grambling (where he succeeded Eddie Robinson), to his current post as personnel executive for the Tampa Bay Buccaneers. It was no easy haul, but Doug weathered it with the same intelligence and grace he brought to his days at quarterback.

Doug Williams: When I was trying to figure out how to get my foot in the door, I called Jim Finks in New Orleans. During our meeting, he made this statement that was shocking. But I respect him, bless his soul, because he was honest. He said, "Doug, you're going to have a problem getting a job in this league. I've always respected you, man. You've always been a straight shooter. But a lot of people will not want you around because they feel threatened by you."

The good thing about being here in Tampa: John Gruden doesn't feel threatened—I've known John since he was fifteen—and Bruce Allen is a straight shooter. I've also got to take my hat off to Tom Coughlin, because Tom Coughlin hired me to be a scout for the Jaguars in 1995. When I left to take the head coaching job at Morehouse, he was going to put me in the front office.

Nearly forty years after his historic first start, Marlin Briscoe keeps right on defying expectations. Clean and sober since 1990, he lives in Long Beach, California, where he owns a mini-storage company and serves as the branch director of the local Boys & Girls Club. In his spare time, he coaches high school football. In 2006, Nike launched an ad campaign in his honor, documenting the highlights of the football program at the fictional Marlin Briscoe High. Michael Vick played the quarterback.

Marlin Briscoe: I went to jail for possession. I never robbed anybody. I never did anything physical to support my habit. I served ninety days twice. The second time, I said, "This is it." When I got out, I had to walk right through the section in San Diego where I used to buy drugs. Lance Alworth had given me $500. I had $500, I'm walking through a drug area, and I'm still a junkie. Ninety days isn't going to cure you. But I said no more. I got through it. A friend came and got me and drove me back to L.A. I resurrected my life, started coaching, took baby steps, one day at a time. Now I have more than I ever had. All the things I lost, I got back—and more.

Progress has been made, but the struggle continues for total acceptance of African-American quarterbacks as not just "athletes," but as the leaders and the faces of their respective teams. From Fritz Pollard to Vince Young, talent and perseverance have overwhelmed resistance; African-American quarterbacks have become the soul of the game.

ACKNOWLEDGMENTS

Thanks to the original Field Generals—James Harris, Marlin Briscoe, Doug Williams, Warren Moon, and Jay Walker—for sharing personal, often painful stories of overcoming. Thanks to David Cummings, Reggie Roberts, Harvey Green. Thanks to Chris Raymond for a heroic—and Herculean—job of editing.

Thanks to Rohena Miller of Niche Marketing for helping to jumpstart the project and for keeping it going. Thanks to Keith Clinkscales, Geoff Reiss, and Gary Hoenig for believing in it from the start. Thanks to Michael MacCambridge for sharing his considerable knowledge of football history and for his advice on the manuscript.

Thanks to Michael Agovino, Jason Catania, Andrew Chaikivsky, Rob Cowen, Dave Chamberlin, Nigel Goodman, Mary Jo Kinser, Eddie Matz, Doug McIntyre, Bryan Mealer, Daniel Rosen, Michael Solomon, Darrell Trimble, and Glen Waggoner for research and direction. Thanks to Roger Jackson, Dan Galvin, Matthew Cole, Charles Curtis, and Michael Mott for fact-checking assistance.

Thanks to Henry Lee for the design. Thanks to Tina Bliss, Mary Sexton, and John Glenn for turning words into type. Thanks to Lori Mason of the Jaguars for all of the scheduling and communications help.

Thanks to the ESPN Books team—Sandy DeShong, Jessica Welke, Ellie Seifert, and Linda Ng—for every effort on my behalf. Thanks to Steven Horne, Roseann Marulli, Margaret McNicol Robbins, and Beth Adelman for reading every word.

And thanks to Keith Hunter, Clinton Jackson, and Lloyd Vance for their enthusiasm and support for the project.

APPENDIX: HONOR ROLL

The drive to equality may have started with Fritz Pollard, but hundreds of athletes worked to level the playing field at quarterback. Below you will find a list (as near to complete as possible) of the African-American men who lettered at quarterback in Division I through 2006.

Last Name	First Name	School	Years
Johnson	Mike	Akron	1988-1989
Washington	James	Akron	1997-2000
Lewis	Walter	Alabama	1980-1983
Zow	Andrew	Alabama	1998-2001
Aaron	Jeff	UAB	2000-2001
Cox	Thomas	UAB	1999-2002
Hackney	Darrell	UAB	2002-2005
Williams	Chris	UAB	2003-2006
Williams	Richie	Appalachian State	2002-2005
Fulcher	Mark	Arizona	1980-1981
Hill	Bruce	Arizona	1973-1975
Jenkins	Alfred	Arizona	1983-1986
Jenkins	Ortege	Arizona	1997-2000
Veal	Ronald	Arizona	1988-1990
Hurst	Grady	Arizona State	1970-1971
McGee	Garrick	Arizona State	1992
Adams	Gary	Arkansas	1989-1991
Burks	Pete	Arkansas	1995-1996
Forte	Rod	Arkansas	1984-1985
Grovey	Quinn	Arkansas	1987-1990
Jackson	Tavaris	Arkansas	2002
Johnson	Robert	Arkansas	2004-2006
Reed	Robert	Arkansas	1994
Thomas	Greg	Arkansas	1984-1987
Lemon	Cleo	Arkansas State	1999-2002
Hollins	Devin	Arkansas State	2002-2005
Allem	Bryan	Army	1980-1982
Crawford	Tory	Army	1985-1987
Goff	Johnny	Army	1997-1998
McMillan	Willie	Army	1989-1991
McWilliams	Bryan	Army	1987-1990
Nevels	Reggie	Army	2001-2004
Williams	Myreon	Army	1990-1991
Booker	Calvin	Auburn	2005

Last Name	First Name	School	Years
Campbell	Jason	**Auburn**	2001-2004
Collier	Meiko	**Auburn**	1998
Craig	Dameyune	**Auburn**	1994-1997
Slack	Reggie	**Auburn**	1986-1989
Thomas	Charles	**Auburn**	1978-1981
Tillman	Allen	**Auburn**	2000-2001
Washington	Pat	**Auburn**	1983-1985
Hill	Talmadge	**Ball State**	2000-2003
Howard	Thomas	**Ball State**	1984
Alford	Jermaine	**Baylor**	1995-1996,1998-1999
Dixon	Kerry	**Baylor**	2000
James	Odell	**Baylor**	1997-1999
Joe	J.J.	**Baylor**	1990-1993
Parks	Terrance	**Baylor**	2004-2005
Rice	Allen	**Baylor**	1982-1983
Robinson	Adrian	**Baylor**	1993-1995
Hicks	Willie	**Boston College**	1988-1990
Harris	Josh	**Bowling Green**	2002-2003
Jacobs	Omar	**Bowling Green**	2003-2005
Turner	Anthony	**Bowling Green**	2004
Washington	Jason	**Bowling Green**	2005-present
Clark	Danny	**Brown**	1987-1989
Coleman	Dennis	**Brown**	1973-1975
Ross	Dante	**Bucknell**	2005
Trigg	Marcello	**Bucknell**	2006
Wilson	Darius	**Bucknell**	2001-2004
Robertson	Reggie	**California**	2001-2004
Garnett	Anthony	**Cal Poly SLO**	2004-2005
Henry	Chad	**Cal Poly SLO**	1998
Bonner	Sherdrick	**Cal State Northridge**	1987-1990
Brady	Marcus	**Cal State Northridge**	1998-2001
Scott	Damone	**Cal State Northridge**	1991
Jones	Khari	**UC Davis**	1991-1993
Bolden	Bill	**UCLA**	1967-1969
Quarles	Bernard	**UCLA**	1979
Washington	Kenny	**UCLA**	1937-1939
Stallworth	Brian	**Central Arkansas**	2001
Turner	Victor	**Central Arkansas**	1984-1987
Young	Henry	**Central Arkansas**	2000-2003
Culpepper	Daunte	**Central Florida**	1995-1998
Jones	Rudy	**Central Florida**	1988-1990
Moffett	Steven	**Central Florida**	2003-present
Sumner	Brandon	**Central Florida**	2004
Carruthers	Marcelle	**Central Michigan**	1986-1987
Smith	Kent	**Central Michigan**	2002, 2004-2005

Last Name	First Name	School	Years
Vickers	Derrick	**Central Michigan**	2000-2003
Kennar	Deontay	**Cincinnati**	1997-2000
Plummer	Chad	**Cincinnati**	1995-1998
Simmons	Willie	**Citadel**	2003
Dantzler	Woody	**Clemson**	1998-2001
Greene	Nealon	**Clemson**	1994-1997
Jordan	Homer	**Clemson**	1980-1982
McCleon	Dexter	**Clemson**	1993-1996
Moncrief	Walter	**Clemson**	1990-1993
Sapp	Patrick	**Clemson**	1994-1995
Solomon	Louis	**Clemson**	1992-1995
Brown	Chris	**Colgate**	2001-2004
Davis	Charles	**Colorado**	1978-1981
Hagan	Darian	**Colorado**	1988-1991
Hatcher	Mark	**Colorado**	1984-1987
Jackson	Bernard	**Colorado**	2006
Johnson	Charles S.	**Colorado**	1988-1990
Stewart	Kordell	**Colorado**	1991-1994
Walters	Marc	**Colorado**	1986
Williams	David	**Colorado**	1973-1975
Hamlett	Leo	**Delaware**	1993-1996
Bryant	D.	**Duke**	2000-2001
Clinkscale	Brent	**Duke**	1980-1982
Driskell	Stanley	**Duke**	1977-1979
Dunn	Mike	**Duke**	1975-1978
Green	David	**Duke**	1996-1997
Jones	Marcus	**Duke**	2005-2006
Lewis	Thaddeus	**Duke**	2006
Sally	Ron	**Duke**	1981, 1984
Alston	Richard	**East Carolina**	1999-2002
Anderson	Michael	**East Carolina**	1991-1992
Blake	Jeff	**East Carolina**	1988-1991
Garrard	David	**East Carolina**	1998-2001
Green	Leander	**East Carolina**	1977-1979
Hester	Chris	**East Carolina**	1993
Hunter	Travis	**East Carolina**	1986-1989
Ingram	Kevin	**East Carolina**	1981-1983
Jones	Ron	**East Carolina**	1984-1987
Nelson	Carlton	**East Carolina**	1979-1982
Pinkney	James	**East Carolina**	1003-2006
Robinson	Desmond	**East Carolina**	2002-2004
Speed	Darrell	**East Carolina**	1982-1985
Tinnen	Ernest	**East Carolina**	1995-1998
Whitaker	Orlando	**East Carolina**	1991
Batch	Charlie	**Eastern Michigan**	1994-1997

Last Name	First Name	School	Years
Brown	Johnelle	**Florida**	1979-1982
Dickey	Gavin	**Florida**	2004-2005
Douglas	Donald	**Florida**	1989
Gaffney	Don	**Florida**	1973-1975
Leak	Chris	**Florida**	2003-2006
LeCount	Terry	**Florida**	1975-1977
Young	Tyrone	**Florida**	1979-1982
McPherson	Adrian	**Florida State**	2001
Ward	Charlie	**Florida State**	1989-1993
Claiborne	Adrian	**Fresno State**	1993-1994
Carter	Quincy	**Georgia**	1998-2000
Jackson	James	**Georgia**	1984-1987
Johnson	Wayne	**Georgia**	1985-1988
Shockley	D.J.	**Georgia**	2002-2006
Ward	Hines	**Georgia**	1995
Bostick	Charles	**Georgia Southern**	1991-1995
Foster	Jason	**Georgia Southern**	2005
Gross	Raymond	**Georgia Southern**	1987-1990
Revere	J.R.	**Georgia Southern**	1998-2001
Robinson	Kenny	**Georgia Southern**	1994-1997
Smiley	Darius	**Georgia Southern**	2003-2005
Williams	Chaz	**Georgia Southern**	2001-2004
Ball	Reggie	**Georgia Tech**	2003-2006
Bilbo	Damarius	**Georgia Tech**	2002
Davis	Donnie	**Georgia Tech**	1992-1995
Hamilton	Joe	**Georgia Tech**	1996-1999
Jones	Shawn	**Georgia Tech**	1989-1992
Foster	Roderic	**Harvard**	1970-1972
Lazarre-White	Adam	**Harvard**	1989-1990
McClusky	John	**Harvard**	1964-1965
Phillips	Neil	**Harvard**	1986-1988
Carter	Michael	**Hawaii**	1990-1993
Cherry	Raphel	**Hawaii**	1981-1984
Glover	Rodney	**Hawaii**	1992-1995
Jasper	Ivin	**Hawaii**	1991-1993
Jones	Warren	**Hawaii**	1985, 1987-1988
Quarles	Bernard	**Hawaii**	1981-1982
Brown	Kharon	**Hofstra**	1993-1995
Butler	Rocky	**Hofstra**	1997-2001
Clarkson	Anton	**Hofstra**	2003-2006
Garay	Carlos	**Hofstra**	1992-1994
Moss	Rhory	**Hofstra**	1987-1990
Yates	Cory	**Hofstra**	2005-present
Botts	Torrence	**Houston**	2001-2002
Brown	Delrick	**Houston**	1977-1979

Last Name	First Name	School	Years
Chinn	Brent	**Houston**	1980
Davis	Danny	**Houston**	1976-1978
Douglas	Donald	**Houston**	1991-1993
Elston	Terry	**Houston**	1979-1980
Landry	Gerald	**Houston**	1983-1986
Nealy	Barrick	**Houston**	2002
Ware	Andre	**Houston**	1987-1989
Wilson	Lionel	**Houston**	1981-1983
Johnson	Johnny	**Illinois**	1993-1995
McCullough	Lawrence	**Illinois**	1978-1979
Meyers	Mel	**Illinois**	1959-1960
Williams	Isiah "Juice"	**Illinois**	2006-present
Anderson	Lester	**Illinois State**	1995-1996
Chaney	Brian	**Illinois State**	1989-1990
Glenn	Kevin	**Illinois State**	1997-2000
Scott	Eric	**Illinois State**	1972-1974
Jones	Terry	**Indiana**	1974-1976
Jones Jr.	Willie	**Indiana**	1973-1975
Lewis	Kellen	**Indiana**	2006-present
Moore	Woody	**Indiana**	1960-1962
Randle El	Antwaan	**Indiana**	1998-2001
Taliaferro	George	**Indiana**	1945, 1947-1948
Banks	Brad	**Iowa**	2001-2002
Gilliam	Frank	**Iowa**	1953-1956
Hollis	Wilburn	**Iowa**	1959-1961
Manson	Jason	**Iowa**	2003-2006
Highsmith	Terrance	**Iowa State**	2004-2005
Meyer	Bret	**Iowa State**	2004-present
Terry	Waye	**Iowa State**	2003
Wallace	Seneca	**Iowa State**	2001-2002
Gordon	Corky	**Jacksonville State**	1991-1994
Kirby	Montressa	**Jacksonville State**	1995-1998
Mullins	Maurice	**Jacksonville State**	2002-2005
Stancil	Reggie	**Jacksonville State**	1999-2002
Kinsey	Mario	**Kansas**	2001
Preston	Asheiki	**Kansas**	1993-1994
Smith	Dylen	**Kansas**	1999-2000
Swanson	Jason	**Kansas**	2004-2005
Thomas	Fred	**Kansas**	1992
Williams	Mark	**Kansas**	1994-1995
Arreguin	Max	**Kansas State**	1968-1970
Bailey	Arthur	**Kansas State**	1974
Beasley	Jonathan	**Kansas State**	1996-1997,1999-2000
Bishop	Michael	**Kansas State**	1997-1998
Freeman	Josh	**Kansas State**	2006-present

Last Name	First Name	School	Years
Roberson	Ell	**Kansas State**	2000-2003
Webb	Allen	**Kansas State**	2004-2005
Williams	Randy	**Kansas State**	1984-1985
Cribbs	Joshua	**Kent State**	2001-2004
Davis	Jose	**Kent State**	1997-1999
Young	Patrick	**Kent State**	1984-1988
Boyd	Shane	**Kentucky**	2001-2004
Abrams	Vernard	**La Salle**	2004
Hall	Brant	**Lehigh**	2000-2002
Threatt	Sedale	**Lehigh**	2004-present
Chiles	Antwan	**Liberty**	1993-1995
Freeman	James	**UL Lafayette**	1990-1992
Hayes	Tyjuan	**UL Lafayette**	1990-1992
Henry	Roy	**UL Lafayette**	1968-1970
King	Thomas	**UL Lafayette**	1985-1988
Mitchell	Brian	**UL Lafayette**	1986-1989
Wallace	Don	**UL Lafayette**	1981-1984
Jyles	Steven	**UL Monroe**	2002-2005
Lancaster	Kinsmon	**UL Monroe**	2006-present
Philyaw	Raymond	**UL Monroe**	1993-1996
Davey	Rohan	**LSU**	1999-2001
Perrilloux	Ryan	**LSU**	2005-present
Randall	Marcus	**LSU**	2002-2004
Russell	JaMarcus	**LSU**	2004-present
Trimble	Carl Otis	**LSU**	1974-1976
Tyler	Herb	**LSU**	1995-1998
Roberts	Kyle	**Louisiana Tech**	2004-2005
Harris	Larry	**Marshall**	1994-1995
Leftwich	Byron	**Marshall**	1998-2002
Morris	Bernard	**Marshall**	2004-present
Nelson	Bud	**Marshall**	1975-1977
Oliver	Reggie	**Marshall**	1971-1973
Payton	Michael	**Marshall**	1990-1992
Evans	Orlando	**Maryland**	2003
Harrison	Latrez	**Maryland**	1999, 2001-2002
Jones	Randall	**Maryland**	1998-1999
McCall	Calvin	**Maryland**	1999-2000
Brooks	Subester	**McNeese State**	1983-1986
Harrison	Freddie	**McNeese State**	1999
Joseph	Kerry	**McNeese State**	1992-1995
Starring	Stephan	**McNeese State**	1979-1982
Anderson	Qadry	**Memphis**	1995-1996
Anglin	Travis	**Memphis**	1999-2002
Avery	Maurice	**Memphis**	2002, 2005
Benton	Keith	**Memphis**	1990-1991

Last Name	First Name	School	Years
Evans	Kenton	**Memphis**	1998
Martin	Darrell	**Memphis**	1979-1982
Odden	Bernard	**Memphis**	1995-1997
Patterson	Lloyd	**Memphis**	1975-1978
Smith	Tom	**Memphis**	1981-1983
Collins	Ryan	**Miami**	1992-1995
Crudup	Derrick	**Miami**	2001-2004
Kelley	Kenny	**Miami**	1998-1999
Bass	Antonio	**Michigan**	2005
Brown	Demetrius	**Michigan**	1987-1988
Franklin	Dennis	**Michigan**	1972-1974
Gonzales	Jermaine	**Michigan**	2001-2004
Johnson	Stacy	**Michigan**	1976
Taylor	Michael	**Michigan**	1987-1989
Baggett	Charlie	**Michigan State**	1973-1975
Banks	Tony	**Michigan State**	1994-1995
Dowdell	Damon	**Michigan State**	2001-2004
McAllister	Bobby (Robert)	**Michigan State**	1985-1988
Raye	Jimmy	**Michigan State**	1965-1967
Thrower	Willie	**Michigan State**	1952
Triplett	Bill	**Michigan State**	1968-1969
Willingham	Tyrone	**Michigan State**	1973-1974
Harris	Josh	**Middle Tennessee State**	2003-2005
Hines	Andrico	**Middle Tennessee State**	2002-2003
Abdul-Khaliq	Asad	**Minnesota**	2000-2003
Avery	Wendell	**Minnesota**	1977-1979
Cockerham	Billy	**Minnesota**	1997-1999
Curry	Craig	**Minnesota**	1969-1971
Dungy	Tony	**Minnesota**	1974-1976
Fleetwood	Marquel	**Minnesota**	1989-1992
Foggie	Rickey	**Minnesota**	1984-1987
Holt	Alan	**Minnesota**	1986-1988
Stephens	Sandy	**Minnesota**	1959-1961
Adams	Lawrence	**Mississippi**	1992-1993
Coleman	Roy	**Mississippi**	1978-1979
Davis	Steven	**Mississippi**	1990-1991
Miller	Romaro	**Mississippi**	1997-2000
Osgood	Chris	**Mississippi**	1985-1986
Schaeffer	Brent	**Mississippi**	2004-present
Spurlock	Michael	**Mississippi**	2003-2004
Barkum	Melvin	**Mississippi State**	1972-1974
Conner	Omarr	**Mississippi State**	2003-present
Madkin	Wayne	**Mississippi State**	1998-2001
Plump	Greg	**Mississippi State**	1991-1993
Robinson	Sleepy	**Mississippi State**	1990-1992

Last Name	First Name	School	Years
Smith	Don	**Mississippi State**	1983-1986
Taite	Derrick	**Mississippi State**	1993-1996
Williams	Albert	**Mississippi State**	1987-1990
Bradley	Phil	**Missouri**	1977-1980
Gage	Justin	**Missouri**	1999
Jones	Corby	**Missouri**	1995-1998
Phelps	Garnett	**Missouri**	1967-1968
Smith	Brad	**Missouri**	2002-2005
Dinkins	David	**Morehead (Ky.) State**	1997-2000
Ford	Winston	**Murray (Ky.) State**	1980-1983
Lewis	Jermaine	**Murray (Ky.) State**	1992
Mosby	Butch	**Murray (Ky.) State**	1992-1994
Proctor	Michael	**Murray (Ky.) State**	1984-1987
Rodney	Corey	**Murray (Ky.) State**	1993
Hampton	Brian	**Navy**	2005-present
McCoy	Chris	**Navy**	1995-1997
McIntosh	Gary	**Navy**	1988-1990
Owens	Lamar	**Navy**	2003-2005
Dailey	Joe	**Nebraska**	2004
Frazier	Tommy	**Nebraska**	1992-1995
Gil	Turner	**Nebraska**	1981-1983
Grant	Mike	**Nebraska**	1989-1990, 1992
Joseph	Mickey	**Nebraska**	1988-1991
Lord	Jammal	**Nebraska**	2000-2003
Mason	Nate	**Nebraska**	1980-1983
McCant	Keithen	**Nebraska**	1990-1991
Newcombe	Bobby	**Nebraska**	1997-1998
Taylor	Steven	**Nebraska**	1985-1988
Denson	Jeremy	**New Mexico**	2000
Porterie	Donovan	**New Mexico**	2006-present
Roberts	Chuck	**New Mexico**	1957-1959
Sellers	Donald	**New Mexico**	1995-1996
Burnette	Chuckie	**North Carolina**	1989-1991
Curry	Ronald	**North Carolina**	1998-2001
Dailey	Joe	**North Carolina**	2006-present
Davenport	Oscar	**North Carolina**	1996-1998
Durant	Darian	**North Carolina**	2001-2004
Thomas	Mike	**North Carolina**	1992-1995
Avery	Tol	**North Carolina State**	1980-1892
Barnette	Jamie	**North Carolina State**	1996-1999
Hurt	Byron	**Northeastern**	1988-1991
Lewis	Rhett	**Northeastern**	1974-1975
McIntosh	Garvey	**Northeastern**	1990-1993
Pearl	Clarzell	**Northeastern**	1992-1994
Bridges	Ricky	**Northern Illinois**	1979-1982

Last Name	First Name	School	Years
Davis	Chet	**Northern Illinois**	1935-1938
Foster	Randall	**Northern Illinois**	1996-1997
Jackson	Frisman	**Northern Illinois**	1997, 1999
Robinson	Stacey	**Northern Illinois**	1989-1990
Taylor	Darryl	**Northern Illinois**	1983, 1985-1986
Taylor	Marshall	**Northern Illinois**	1985-1988
Williams	Kenneth	**Northern Illinois**	1995
Williams	Len	**Northwestern**	1990-1993
Battle	Arnez	**Notre Dame**	1998-2000
Brown	Clifford	**Notre Dame**	1971-1973
Chappell	Eric	**Notre Dame**	1998
Holiday	Carlyle	**Notre Dame**	2000-2003
Jackson	Jarious	**Notre Dame**	1996-1998
Jones	Demetrius	**Notre Dame**	2006-present
McDougal	Kevin	**Notre Dame**	1992-1993
Rice	Tony	**Notre Dame**	1987-1988
Bevly	Rich	**Ohio**	1972-1974
Bryant	Cleve	**Ohio**	1972-1974
Jackson	Dontrelle	**Ohio**	1999-2002
Ray	Freddie	**Ohio**	2000-2003
Thornton	Anthony	**Ohio**	1987-1990
Wilson	Kareem	**Ohio**	1995-1998
Gerald	Rod	**Ohio State**	1975-1977
Green	Cornelius	**Ohio State**	1973-1975
Jackson	Stanley	**Ohio State**	1995-1997
Smith	Troy	**Ohio State**	2003-present
Bradley	Danny	**Oklahoma**	1981-1984
Brown	Terrence	**Oklahoma**	1993-1996
Daniels	Brandon	**Oklahoma**	1996-1998
Holieway	Jamelle	**Oklahoma**	1985-1988
Jackson	Kerry	**Oklahoma**	1972, 1974
Lott	Thomas	**Oklahoma**	1976-1978
Mitchell	Eric	**Oklahoma**	1985-1988
Moore	Eric	**Oklahoma**	1995-1998
Shephard	Darrell	**Oklahoma**	1980-1981
Thompson	Charles	**Oklahoma**	1987-1988
Thompson	Paul	**Oklahoma**	2003-present
Watts	J.C.	**Oklahoma**	1978-1980
Bailey	Harold	**Oklahoma State**	1976-1979
Jones	Tone	**Oklahoma State**	1993-1996
Lindsay	Tony	**Oklahoma State**	1997-2000
Reid	Bobby	**Oklahoma State**	2005-present
Williams	Ronnie	**Oklahoma State**	1985-1987
Dixon	Dennis	**Oregon**	2005-present
Ogburn	Reggie	**Oregon**	1979-1980

Last Name	First Name	School	Years
Robinson	Robert	**Oregon**	1927-1929
Singleton	Herb	**Oregon**	1973
Smith	Akili	**Oregon**	1997-1998
Alexander	Tim	**Oregon State**	1995-1997
Bryant	Terrance	**Oregon State**	1997-1998
Muhammad	Rahim	**Oregon State**	1993-1996
Shanklin	Don	**Oregon State**	1994-1996
Glover	Malcolm	**Pennsylvania**	1988-1989
Casey	Rashard	**Penn State**	1998-2000
Clark	Darryll	**Penn State**	2006-present
Cooper	Mike	**Penn State**	1968-1970
Richardson	Wally	**Penn State**	1992, 1994-1996
Robinson	Michael	**Penn State**	2002-2005
Dickerson	Darnell	**Pittsburgh**	1987-1988,1990
Dinkins	Darnell	**Pittsburgh**	1996-1999
Ford	Henry	**Pittsburgh**	1951-1954
Haygood	Robert	**Pittsburgh**	1973-1976
Rutherford	Rod	**Pittsburgh**	2000-2003
Harvey	Brock	**Princeton**	1994-1995
Plummer	Rod	**Princeton**	1968-1971
Hunter	Eric	**Purdue**	1989-1992
Armstrong	Joel	**Rice**	2004-2005
Calhoun	Mike	**Rice**	1981-1982
Emanuel	Bert	**Rice**	1992-1993
Evans	Corey	**Rice**	1998, 2000-2001
Hurd	Jeremy	**Rice**	2000
Overton	Kerry	**Rice**	1983-1986
Reed	Claude	**Rice**	1973-1976
Roper	Quentis	**Rice**	1985-1988
Vincent	Stahle	**Rice**	1969-1971
Gustus	Shawn	**Richmond**	1998-2001
Miles	Jimmie	**Richmond**	1995-1999
Spinner	Bryson	**Richmond**	2003
Tutt	Stacy	**Richmond**	2001-2005
Lucas	Ray	**Rutgers**	1992-1995
McMichael	Eddie	**Rutgers**	1978-1980
Tarver	Tom	**Rutgers**	1989-1991
Johnson	Josh	**San Diego**	2004-present
Allen	Doug	**San Jose State**	1984-1985
Crooks	Brennan	**San Jose State**	1999-2000
Heffner	Antonio	**South Carolina**	2005
Jenkins	Corey	**South Carolina**	2001-2002
Newton	Syvelle	**South Carolina**	2003-present
Pinkins	Dondrail	**South Carolina**	2002-2004
Wright	Anthony	**South Carolina**	1995-1998

Last Name	First Name	School	Years
Banks	Ronnie	**South Florida**	2001-2004
Blackwell	Marquel	**South Florida**	1999-2002
Denson	Courtney	**South Florida**	2005
Julmiste	Pat	**South Florida**	2003-present
King	Don	**SMU**	1982-1985
Phillips	Chris	**SMU**	2003-2006
Wesson	Ricky	**SMU**	1973-1976
Willis	Justin	**SMU**	2006-present
Anderson	Andrew	**Southern Mississippi**	1983-1986
Carter	Damion	**Southern Mississippi**	2003
Carter	Simmie	**Southern Mississippi**	1987
Collier	Reggie	**Southern Mississippi**	1979-1982
Ducksworth	Robert	**Southern Mississippi**	1982-1985
Hightower	Aaron	**Southern Mississippi**	1992
Windsor	Chris	**Southern Mississippi**	1995-1996
Young	Ailrick	**Southern Mississippi**	1987-1988
Young	Jeremy	**Southern Mississippi**	2004-2005
Lewls	Chris	**Stanford**	2000-2003
Anderson	Robin "R.J."	**Syracuse**	2000-2003
Fields	Joe	**Syracuse**	2004-2005
Graves	Marvin	**Syracuse**	1990-1993
Mason	Kevin	**Syracuse**	1992-1994
McNabb	Donovan	**Syracuse**	1995-1998
McPherson	Don	**Syracuse**	1985-1987
Patterson	Perry	**Syracuse**	2003-present
Sidat-Singh	Wilmeth	**Syracuse**	1937-1938
Batteaux	Patrick	**TCU**	1996-1999
Clay	Leon	**TCU**	1989-1992
Gulley	Anthony	**TCU**	1982-1984
Hassell	Brandon	**TCU**	2003-2004
Jiles	Ron	**TCU**	1986-1989
Jones	Reuben	**TCU**	1980-1982
Printers	Casey	**TCU**	1999-2001
Taylor	Fred	**TCU**	1996
Bonner	Pat	**Temple**	1995-1997
Burris	Henry	**Temple**	1993-1996
Harvey	Kevin	**Temple**	1997-1998
Nuckerson	Greg	**Temple**	1998
Richardson	Anthony	**Temple**	1989-1991
Scott	Devin	**Temple**	1998-2001
Thompson	James	**Temple**	1984-1986
Washington	Walter	**Temple**	2003-2004
Banks	James	**Tennessee**	2002
Colquitt	Jerry	**Tennessee**	1991-1994
Henton	Sterling	**Tennessee**	1987,1989-1990

Last Name	First Name	School	Years
Holloway	Condredge	**Tennessee**	1972-1974
Leak	C.J.	**Tennessee**	2002-2004
Martin	Tee	**Tennessee**	1996-1999
Robinson	Tony	**Tennessee**	1983-1985
Schaeffer	Brent	**Tennessee**	2004
Streater	Jimmy	**Tennessee**	1977-1979
Brown	James	**Texas**	1994-1997
Forbes	Donovan	**Texas**	1986, 1989
Little	Donnie	**Texas**	1978-1980
Young	Vince	**Texas**	2003-2005
Dewalt	Roy	**UT Arlington**	1975-1979
Carter	Jason	**Texas A&M**	2002
McNeal	Reggie	**Texas A&M**	2002-2005
Murray	Kevin	**Texas A&M**	1983-1986
Osgood	Chris	**Texas A&M**	1988-1989
Hygh	John	**Texas State**	1991-1994
Nealy	Barrick	**Texas State**	2003-2005
Price	Gilbert	**Texas State**	1988-1991
Wynn	Spergon	**Texas State**	1998-1999
Hall	Robert	**Texas Tech**	1990-1993
Lethridge	Zebbie	**Texas Tech**	1994-1997
Bolden	Tavares	**Toledo**	1999-2001
Ealey	Chuck	**Toledo**	1969-1971
Hall	Maurice	**Toledo**	1978-1981
Kelso	Jim	**Toledo**	1980-1983
Wallace	Chris	**Toledo**	1997-1998
Davis	Stan	**Troy**	1993-1996
Foster	Julian	**Troy**	2005-present
Haugabook	Omar	**Troy**	2006-present
Leak	Aaron	**Troy**	2003-2004
McDowell	D.T.	**Troy**	2004
Simmons	Kelvin	**Troy**	1991-1993
Hall	Nickie	**Tulane**	1977-1980
Jones	Terrence	**Tulane**	1985-1988
Joseph	Derrick	**Tulane**	2002
King	Shaun	**Tulane**	1995-1998
Ricard	Lester	**Tulane**	2003-present
Smith	Deron	**Tulane**	1989-1990
DeGar	Troy	**Tulsa**	1995-1996
Jackson	Kenny	**Tulsa**	1978-1981
Pearson	Drew	**Tulsa**	1970
Stripling	Mike	**Tulsa**	1966-1968
Bowen	Eugene	**UNLV**	1985-1986
Brown	Jared	**UNLV**	1994-1995
Cooper	Hunkie	**UNLV**	1990-1991

Last Name	First Name	School	Years
Cunningham	Randall	**UNLV**	1982-1984
Hinds	Rocky	**UNLV**	2006-present
King	Sam	**UNLV**	1979, 1981
Laney	Calvin	**UNLV**	1984-1985
Price	Charles	**UNLV**	1988-1989
Sims	Scott	**UNLV**	1987-1989
Thomas	Jason	**UNLV**	2000-2002
Wallace	Genet	**UNLV**	1982-1983
Evans	Vince	**USC**	1974-1976
Jones	Jimmy	**USC**	1969-1971
Peete	Rodney	**USC**	1985-1988
Perry	Reggie	**USC**	1991-1993
Wood	Willie	**USC**	1957-1959
Woods	Quincy	**USC**	1997
Arceaneaux	Darnell	**Utah**	1997-2000
Johnson	Brian	**Utah**	2004-present
Stevens	Mark	**Utah**	1983-1984
Jackson III	Leon	**Utah State**	2004-present
Gray	Shawn	**UTEP**	1991-1994
Lunnon	Gerred	**UTEP**	2000-2001
Allen	Damian	**Vanderbilt**	1995-1997
Carter	Jamail	**Vanderbilt**	1996
Culley	David	**Vanderbilt**	1976
Douglas	Cedrick	**Vanderbilt**	1993
Fuller	Ardell	**Vanderbilt**	1981-1982
Heflin	Van	**Vanderbilt**	1978-1979
Jones	Eric	**Vanderbilt**	1986-1988
Nickson	Chris	**Vanderbilt**	2005-present
Simon	Kenny	**Vanderbilt**	1995
Wilson	Marcus	**Vanderbilt**	1991-1994
Burroughs	Marvin	**Villanova**	2003-present
Brooks	Aaron	**Virginia**	1996-1998
Davis	Harrison	**Virginia**	1971-1972
Ferguson	Kevin	**Virginia**	1984
Goodman	Bobby	**Virginia**	1991-1992
Hagans	Marques	**Virginia**	2004-2005
Manley	Ted	**Virginia**	1980
Moore	Shawn	**Virginia**	1987-1990
Spinner	Bryson	**Virginia**	2000-2001
Willis	Symmion	**Virginia**	1993-1994
Chapman	Erik	**Virginia Tech**	1986-1987
Clark	Al	**Virginia Tech**	1995-1998
DeShazo	Maurice	**Virginia Tech**	1992-1994
Holt	Cory	**Virginia Tech**	2005-present
Randall	Bryan	**Virginia Tech**	2001-2004

Last Name	First Name	School	Years
Rogers	Phil	**Virginia Tech**	1975
Vick	Marcus	**Virginia Tech**	2003, 2005
Vick	Michael	**Virginia Tech**	1999-2000
Barnhill	Phil	**Wake Forest**	1989-1990
Dolder	Adam	**Wake Forest**	1994
Everett	Solomon	**Wake Forest**	1974-1976
Leak	C.J.	**Wake Forest**	1999
Randolph	Cory	**Wake Forest**	2002-2005
Sankey	Ben	**Wake Forest**	1996-1999
Summers	Freddie	**Wake Forest**	1967-1968
Young	Anthony	**Wake Forest**	2000
McBride	Cliff	**Washington**	1976
Moon	Warren	**Washington**	1976-1978
Stanback	Isaiah	**Washington**	2003-present
Blount	Ed	**Washington State**	1984-1986
Turner	Ricky	**Washington State**	1980-1983
Boykin	Eric	**West Virginia**	1994-1996
Brown	Jarrett	**West Virginia**	2006-present
Hales	Charles	**West Virginia**	2003-2004
Harris	Major	**West Virginia**	1987-1989
Jones	Derek	**West Virginia**	2001
Jones	Greg	**West Virginia**	1988, 1990
Marshall	Rasheed	**West Virginia**	2001-2004
Studstill	Darren	**West Virginia**	1990-1993
Talley	John	**West Virginia**	1985-1987
White	Patrick	**West Virginia**	2005-2006
Davis	Willie	**Western Illinois**	1990
Jackson	Frisman	**Western Illinois**	2000
Houston	Daryl	**Western Kentucky**	1994-1995
Jewell	J.J.	**Western Kentucky**	1993-1994
Johnson	Jason	**Western Kentucky**	2000-2001
Malcome	Jairus "Meco"	**Western Kentucky**	1991-1994
Pimpleton	Donte	**Western Kentucky**	1999-2001
Taggart	Willie	**Western Kentucky**	1995-1998
Thompson	Eddie	**Western Kentucky**	1991-1993
McJunkins	Prince	**Wichita State**	1979-1982
Manley	Phil	**Yale**	1980

Compiled with the assistance of Lloyd M. Vance, editor of BQB-Site.com.

In honor of the late, great Willie Thrower, the following list includes the names of every African-American quarterback to attempt at least eight passes in the AFL or the NFL.

Last Name	First Name	Team	Years
Banks	Tony	Baltimore Ravens	1999-2000
		St. Louis Rams	1996-1998
		Dallas Cowboys	2001
		Washington Redskins	2001
		Houston Texans	2002-2005
Batch	Charlie	Detroit Lions	1998-2001
		Pittsburgh Steelers	2002-present
Bishop	Michael	New England Patriots	2000
Blake	Jeff	New York Jets	1992-1993
		Cincinnati Bengals	1994-1999
		New Orleans Saints	2000-2001
		Baltimore Ravens	2002
		Arizona Cardinals	2003
		Philadelphia Eagles	2004
		Chicago Bears	2005
Blount	Ed	San Francisco 49ers	1987
Briscoe	Marlon	Denver Broncos	1968
Brooks	Aaron	New Orleans Saints	2000-2005
		Oakland Raiders	2006-present
Burris	Henry	Chicago Bears	2002
Campbell	Jason	Washington Redskins	2006-present
Carter	Quincy	Dallas Cowboys	2001-2003
		New York Jets	2004
Collier	Reggie	Dallas Cowboys	1986
Craig	Dameyune	Carolina Panthers	2000-2001
Culpepper	Daunte	Minnesota Vikings	1999-2005
		Miami Dolphins	2006-present
Cunningham	Randall	Philadelphia Eagles	1985-1995
		Minnesota Vikings	1997-1999
		Dallas Cowboys	2000-2001
Davey	Rohan	New England Patriots	2002-2004
Dickinson	Parnell	Tampa Bay Buccaneers	1976
Dungy	Tony	Pittsburgh Steelers	1977-1979
Evans	Vince	Chicago Bears	1977-1983
		Los Angeles Raiders	1987-1995
Garrard	David	Jacksonville Jaguars	2002-present
Gilliam	Joe	Pittsburgh Steelers	1972-1975
Gray	Quinn	Jacksonville Jaguars	2003-present
Harris	James	Buffalo Bills	1969-1971
		Los Angeles Rams	1973-1976

Last Name	First Name	Team	Years
		San Diego Chargers	1977-1979
Jackson	Jarious	Denver Broncos	2000-2003
Jones	J.J.	New York Jets	1975
King	Shaun	Tampa Bay Buccaneers	1999-2003
		Arizona Cardinals	2004
Leftwich	Byron	Jacksonville Jaguars	2003-present
Lucas	Ray	New England Patriots	1996
		New York Jets	1997-2000
		Miami Dolphins	2001-2002
Martin	Tee	Oakland Raiders	2003
Mays	Dave	Cleveland Browns	1976-1977
		Buffalo Bills	1978
McNabb	Donovan	Philadelphia Eagles	1999-present
McNair	Steve	Houston Oilers/Tennesee Titans	1994-2005
		Baltimore Ravens	2006-present
Moon	Warren	Houston Oilers	1984-1993
		Minnesota Vikings	1994-1996
		Seattle Seahawks	1997-1998
		Kansas City Chiefs	1999-2000
Moore	Shawn	Denver Broncos	1992
Peete	Rodney	Detroit Lions	1989-1993
		Dallas Cowboys	1994
		Philadelphia Eagles	1995-1997
		Washington Redskins	1999
		Carolina Panthers	2002-2004
Robinson	Tony	Washington Redskins	1987
Smith	Akili	Cincinnati Bengals	1999-2004
Stewart	Kordell	Pittsburgh Steelers	1995-2002
		Chicago Bears	2003
		Baltimore Ravens	2004-2005
Taliaferro	George	Baltimore Colts	1953-1954
		Philadelphia Eagles	1955
Thrower	Willie	Chicago Bears	1953
Totten	Willie	Buffalo Bills	1987
Vick	Michael	Atlanta Falcons	2001-present
Wallace	Seneca	Seattle Seahawks	2003-present
Walton	Johnnie	Philadelphia Eagles	1976-1979
Ware	Andre	Detroit Lions	1990-1993
Williams	Doug	Tampa Bay Buccaneers	1978-1982
		Washington Redskins	1986-1989
Wright	Anthony	Dallas Cowboys	2000-2001
		Baltimore Ravens	2002-2005
Wynn	Spergon	Cleveland Browns	2000
		Minnesota Vikings	2001
Young	Vince	Tennessee Titans	2006-present

EXTRA POINTS

ESPN

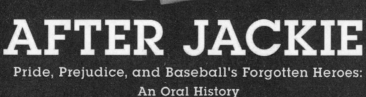

AFTER JACKIE

Pride, Prejudice, and Baseball's Forgotten Heroes:
An Oral History

Cal Fussman

When Jackie Robinson joined the Brooklyn Dodgers in 1947, he forever changed the game of baseball—and America itself. In *After Jackie*, author Cal Fussman traces Robinson's enormous legacy in sports, politics, and the civil rights movement through the men and women who came after him. Through moving and intimate interviews with players of African-American descent such as Hank Aaron, Willie Mays, Frank Robinson, and Bob Gibson, as well as such luminaries as Muhammad Ali, Maya Angelou, Colin Powell, and Walter Cronkite, among others, *After Jackie* recalls the day when one man altered history for so many.

DON NEWCOMBE

(Pitcher, 1949–60)

Why?

Why?

What it is about us that we had to be treated as subhuman beings?

What did we do to be treated like we were treated?

Were they afraid of us?

I'm the only player in baseball history who won the Rookie of the Year award, the Most Valuable Player award, and the Cy Young award. Nobody else in baseball history—black, white, brown, tan, yellow, whatever—has won those three awards in his career.

Was the white man afraid of that?

I could go to the Army, go to war, fight and die for my country like some of my friends did. This country took my taxes. But I couldn't play the national pastime. Bitter? Oh, yeah, we were bitter.

Jackie always said that one day we're going to change the spelling and the meaning of the word "bitter." We're going to replace the "i" with an "e" and make it "better."

That's why we have to go through all this, he used to say, to change that "i" to an "e."

◆ ◆ ◆

The Philadelphia Phillies had a coach who was a real race-baiter. He'd sit in the corner of the dugout calling us all kinds of names, from the first inning on.

One day he was at it at Ebbets Field, and Jackie came over to the mound. Jackie said, "Newk, you hear what he's saying to us."

I said, "Sure, Jack, I'm closer to him than you are."

"What are you going to do about it?"

I said, "Wait until Ennis comes up. [Del Ennis was the Phillies' best hitter.] When he comes up, I'll undress his ass."

Jackie nodded and said, "If he comes out to the mound, give him to me. Don't you get into it. Just give him to me. I want him."

And when Ennis came up, that's what I did—I undressed him on the first pitch with a fastball, high and tight.

Del got up, brushed his uniform off, and put his bat down. He then turned back toward the dugout, walked over a couple of steps, and said something to that dude sitting in the corner.

We didn't know what he said, but he came back out to the plate. I struck him out, and that was that.

Years later, when I was with the Cincinnati Reds, I played with Del, and I asked him what he'd said to that SOB that day in the dugout in Ebbets Field.

Del said, "I told the sonofabitch to shut his mouth and leave you alone or I was gonna pull his tongue out. He didn't have to go out there and hit against you."

MONTE IRVIN

(Outfielder, 1949–56)

One afternoon we were traveling in Alabama, from Montgomery to Birmingham. It was hot as hell, and we came to this café that was built on a terrace. We pulled the bus off the road, and a few of us got out. A white lady was serving people, and when she saw us, she started shakin' her head.

I said, "Why you shakin' your head, Ma'am? You don't even know what we want."

She said, "I don't give a damn. Whatever you want, I don't have any. The answer is no."

"Well," I said, "that's too bad, because we only wanted to buy a hamburger or a hot dog or something. But mainly what we wanted was a cool glass of water."

"I'm not going to sell you anything," she said. "If you want some water, there's a well in the back."

So we went back to the well and hoisted up a bucket of water. There was a gourd nearby. We drank from this gourd, then walked back to the bus to head on down the road.

When I looked back, I saw this woman out by the well, smashing the gourd that we'd drunk out of into little pieces.

BOB VEALE

(PITCHER, 1962–74)

A guy I know went into this restaurant, and they told him. "We don't serve niggers here." And my friend said, "I hadn't planned on ordering any niggers. And I don't want no Crackers, neither. All I want is a steak sandwich."

BUCK O'NEIL

(Negro Leagues first baseman and manager, 1937–55)

One of the saddest moments in my life might have been at a pageant in Sarasota when I was young. Every year this pageant would have a parade. On this one day, they got four of us black boys, had us pull off our shirts, and they painted our bodies.

The idea was for a white boy and a white girl to be carried through the streets on a chariot. There were two long poles at the bottom of the chariot, and the four of us were at each end of the poles—four black slave bearers carrying a white king and queen.

We're walking down Main Street and everybody in Sarasota is lined up watching. Then I look over and see that my friends are lookin' at me.

When it was over I got back to school and cried. Mrs. Booker, my teacher, comforted me, told me she knew just how I felt. But I gotta tell you, it took me a long time to get over that.

Many years later, I was playing with the Memphis Red Sox of the Negro Leagues when I ran into Charlie Henry, who was there promoting the Zulu Cannibal Giants. The Zulu Cannibal Giants painted their faces, put rings through their noses, and took the field in straw skirts. They dressed like they were out of a Tarzan movie to attract a crowd—and they sure did attract a crowd.

Anyway, Charlie Henry said to me, "How much you makin'?"

I said, "About $90 a month."

He says, "I can get you more than that if you join the Zulu Cannibal Giants. We're going up north to Canada."

In those days, jumping around from team to team was how it was. We never had any written contracts. The money Charlie Henry was offering was too good to pass up, so I decided to go.

Well, we got to Canada, and I put on that damn straw dress. I went out on the field, and at first I was thinking, I'm not in America, and none of my people can see me. But I looked around at all these white Canadian people, and they're looking at me like I just came right out of the bush.

AFTER JACKIE

The idea was for a white boy and a white girl to be carried through the streets on a chariot. There were two long poles at the bottom of the chariot, and the four of us were at each end of the poles—four black slave bearers carrying a white king and queen.

We're walking down Main Street and everybody in Sarasota is lined up watching. Then I look over and see that my friends are lookin' at me.

When it was over I got back to school and cried. Mrs. Booker, my teacher, comforted me, told me she knew just how I felt. But I gotta tell you, it took me a long time to get over that.

Many years later, I was playing with the Memphis Red Sox of the Negro Leagues when I ran into Charlie Henry, who was there promoting the Zulu Cannibal Giants. The Zulu Cannibal Giants painted their faces, put rings through their noses, and took the field in straw skirts. They dressed like they were out of a Tarzan movie to attract a crowd—and they sure did attract a crowd.

Anyway, Charlie Henry said to me, "How much you makin'?"

I said, "About $90 a month."

He says, "I can get you more than that if you join the Zulu Cannibal Giants. We're going up north to Canada."

In those days, jumping around from team to team was how it was. We never had any written contracts. The money Charlie Henry was offering was too good to pass up, so I decided to go.

Well, we got to Canada, and I put on that damn straw dress. I went out on the field, and at first I was thinking, I'm not in America, and none of my people can see me. But I looked around at all these white Canadian people, and they're looking at me like I just came right out of the bush.

At that moment, a feeling came rushing back to me, the same feeling I had as a boy when my friends saw me carrying the white kids through the street. And I said, *Sheeeeeeeee*-it! I'm getting out of here. And this is never gonna happen to me again.

And it didn't.

◆ ◆ ◆

Now, Jackie understood it was about the money.

I left the Monarchs for the service in World War II, but I heard a story about Jackie his first year with the team that made me know he understood.

The Monarchs were traveling through the South on the team bus, and they stopped for gas. It was a big bus with two 50-gallon tanks. Jackie got out and started to go to the rest room, but the white attendant stopped him.

"Where you going?"

Jackie said, "To the rest room."

All the other players were used to segregation, they accepted that they couldn't use the rest room at a white gas station. But not Jackie. He'd come from college in California. He said, "Take the pump out. If I can't go to the bathroom, then you can't sell me any gas."

Now, this white man's thinking something like this: That's a big bus. It's gonna take more gas than I'm gonna sell to any other customer today. If I pull the pump out, I'm gonna lose all that money. So he said to Jackie, "Okay, go to the rest room, but don't stay long."

Yessir, Jackie understood it was about the money.

JAMES EARL JONES

(ACTOR)

When I came out of the Army after Korea I expected there to be a race war. When that didn't happen, when we had opportunities to explore other ways of solving our social problems, I thought God had smiled on the whole nation, that whatever happened afterward was supposed to happen and should have happened sooner.

And it all started with Jackie Robinson.

BILLY WILLIAMS

(Outfielder, 1959–76)

We were headed back from Victoria in the Texas League and we stopped at this restaurant, but they wouldn't let us in to eat. We got back to our place in San Antonio, and I told my roommate, "I'm tired of this shit. Take me to the train station."

He said, "What are you gonna do? Go home?"

I said, "Yes, I am. I'm not putting up with this shit any longer. I'm going back home."

And I took the train and went home to Whistler, Alabama.

I understand what you're thinking: Wasn't it just as bad back in Alabama as it was in Texas? All I can say is, it may be confusing for most people, but it wasn't for me.

See, it was mixed where I grew up. First, you had Sixth Street, which was all black. Next to Sixth Street you had a big field. And on the other side of that field you had Ninth Street, which was white, but not all white. There were two black families who lived on Ninth Street.

We used to play baseball with a kid from one of the black families on Ninth Street. Leon Franklin. He would get some of his white neighbors to play against us. When we went over there we called it a road trip.

Leon's father worked for a fruit distributor, and he'd bring home all kinds of fruit. After we'd play, we'd all go by his house—black and white—sit around, talk baseball, and eat. In that setting, it was natural for black and white to be together.

At the same time, I used to go fishing with my grandfather, and as we'd be coming home we'd want a hamburger or a hot dog. There was this little place that served them up, and my grandfather would walk straight up to the white line. See, he had sandy hair and nobody could tell that he was black. My father's father. I've got pictures at home.

Now, I couldn't get on that white line with him to get a hamburger because I had black skin. So I'd just sit in the car and wait. I realized from my grandfather that skin color has nothing to do with anything. It's all what's in the heart. But I also realized that I couldn't go on that white line.

Confusing? Yeah, I guess so. But I understood where to go and where not to go and how to be comfortable at home in Alabama. In the Texas League, I'd be hungry, and I couldn't eat. You just get fed up with it. When you're out of your environment, somehow it's different.

Anyway, I'd been home four or five days, and all of a sudden from a distance I saw this Ford Fury coming toward the house. And I thought, Oh, I'm in trouble now.

Buck O'Neil always drove a Fury. He was a Cubs scout, and he was gonna want to know why I left the team in San Antonio. But the thing about Buck is, he'd played and managed in the Negro Leagues. He knew how it was. Later I heard that Ernie Banks left for home and that Buck had to go get him.

So Buck came on in with a big smile and said, "Billy, how you doin'?"

I said, "I'm doin' fine."

He didn't even mention what happened in Texas. He acted like he was just dropping by to visit an old friend.

So that evening we got in Buck's Fury and we went down to the local ballpark. The game was going on, and everybody I went to school with was coming over, saying, "Hey, Billy! What are you doing back here? You're a professional baseball player. That must be great. Going around the country, getting paid, and getting meal money."

I couldn't really explain that I couldn't spend my meal money because the white people behind the counters at restaurants wouldn't take it—or even let me in the door.

It didn't take long for me to realize the opportunity that I'd turned my back on. Buck didn't have to say a word. A couple of days later, I said, "Buck, I'm ready to go back."

About that time, the Cubs' general manager, John Holland, sent Rogers Hornsby out to take a look at the talent in the Cubs' minor league system.

Rogers Hornsby was a great hitter, a Hall of Famer, and definitely an old-school kind of guy. He had a reputation for being real crusty. He managed for a while, and I heard a story that when he wanted to change a pitcher, he'd walk to the top step of the dugout, look out to the bullpen, and yell, "You! Come in." Then he'd look to the mound and yell, "You! You're out." Didn't even walk to the mound.

So Hornsby came to look us over. We all worked out, and afterward he sat the entire team in the stands. He started going over all the players, one by one. He'd point to a guy and say, "You! You can go get a job right now. You can't play baseball." Then he'd move on to the next guy and it was the same thing: "You can't play."

Ron Santo and I were scared stiff.

Hornsby got to me and said, "Williams, you can play in the big leagues right now. You can hit in the big leagues. But you've got to learn to play some defense." Then he got to Santo: "You can play some defense. You're gonna get some hits in the big leagues. You two can play. All you other guys can go home and get jobs."

For me, it was a revelation. I don't know what attracted Rogers Hornsby to me. Maybe it was my swing. I know he saw something. And I also know he didn't see something: the color of my skin.

CARL ERSKINE

(Pitcher, 1948–59)

After a game at Ebbets Field, I walked outside to where the families of the players were waiting. Fans were gathered around us. Rachel was there with Jackie Jr., and I went over to say hello and kidded with them. It seemed very natural and I didn't think a thing of it—but Jackie did.

Afterward, he said to me: "Thank you for what you did out there in front of the fans."

What had seemed so normal to me stood out to Jackie in a way that I couldn't grasp. "Jackie," I told him, "you can thank me for pitching a good game. But don't thank me for just being myself."

That kind of amazed Jackie. He said, "You don't have a problem with this race thing, do you?"

There were a couple of guys on the Dodgers from the deep South—Dixie Walker and Bobby Bragan—when Jackie came up. They knew they'd have to go back home and answer to their buddies: Do you shower with this guy? Do you eat with this guy? Do you sleep in the same hotel with this guy? All that was taboo in the South. So they resisted Jackie being there, even asked to be traded. But they were about the only ones.

The way I saw it, there was a pretty quick acceptance from the Dodgers: Jackie was one of us.

ROBERT PAIGE

(Son of Satchel Paige, pitcher, 1948–53, 1965)

It took 20 years before I realized what a historical event it was. At the time I didn't think it was particularly significant. This was back in 1965. We didn't even take a camera to the game.

This is what happened. My dad was going to be put on the Kansas City Athletics roster in order to qualify for his major league pension. He thought he'd spend the time coaching the pitchers and giving advice. He had no idea that they were going to put him in the game—he was 59 years old. But it turned out he needed to pitch three innings to get that pension.

I was 13 or 14 at the time. I'd always heard about what he'd done in baseball, and people were always stopping him for autographs and photographs. So to me it was just Dad being Dad.

But he didn't have much advance notice, and he decided to check on his control out in the yard. I was his "official catcher." Playing catch was something that we did, just like other fathers and sons every weekend throughout America. Only this time it just so happened I was warming up my 59-year-old father to pitch against the Boston Red Sox.

Dad got me all suited up in the catcher's gear—the mask, the chest protector, shin guards, everything. He had this basket of balls that we always used. Dad's philosophy was that we didn't chase balls—the ones that got away just got away.

My father really had to bear down to see what kind of control he had. Must've been about four or five dozen balls in that basket. He'd tell me what he was going to throw. "This is gonna be a curveball—it's gonna break this way. This is gonna be a sinker. This one's gonna have a little speed on it." Just so I'd have an idea what was coming.

We went through that basket of balls and he was quite pleased with his control. We called it quits, and the next day he went out to pitch against the Boston Red Sox.

It was the first time I'd ever seen him in a professional game. Everybody else wondered how a 59-year-old man could possibly play in the major leagues. But I didn't expect anything less than a good performance because of all the stories I'd heard about him.

The crowd was cheering like crazy. A few of the Red Sox made some pretty good contact, but they were flyouts. My dad didn't give up any runs. In three innings, he gave up only one hit—a Carl Yastrzemski double. All the while I was thinking, This is just what Dad does, this is who he is.

His ERA for 1965, when he was 59?

0.00.

DON NEWCOMBE

Do you know what we did? Well, let Martin Luther King tell you.

In 1968, Martin had dinner in my house with my family. This was 28 days before he was assassinated. He said, "Don, I don't know what I would've done without you guys—setting up the minds of people for change. You, Jackie, and Roy will never know how easy you made it for me to do my job."

Can you imagine that?

How easy *we* made it for Martin Luther King?!

AFTER JACKIE will be available
wherever books are sold in April 2007